SUPPORTIVE
ACCOUNTABILITY

How to Inspire
People and Improve
Performance

SYLVIA MELENA

Melena Consulting Group
La Mesa, CA

Published by Melena Consulting Group.

3755 Avocado Blvd. #291
La Mesa, CA 91941
smelena@melenaconsulting.com

Library of Congress Control Number: 2018903952
ISBN: 978-0-9997435-0-8

Disclaimer: The author and publisher make no warranties regarding the completeness and accuracy of the information contained in this book and assume no responsibility for any errors or omissions. The purchase of this book does not establish a consulting relationship with the purchaser or reader. There is no guarantee regarding results. This book is not a substitute for the advice of your organization's human resources professionals, legal counsel, or other designated experts. Every situation is different. To mitigate risk to yourself and your organization, seek advice from your organization's designated experts. The author and publisher assume no liability for damages that may result from the use of the information contained within. The characters, organizations, and events portrayed in this book are fictitious. Any resemblance to real people, events, organizations, or programs is merely coincidental and unintentional.

The Melena Consulting Group logo is a registered trademark of Melena Consulting Group. "Supportive Accountability Leadership," the "Four Leadership Styles of Supportive Accountability," and the "4 P's of Accountability" are trademarks of Melena Consulting Group.

To my husband, daughter, son, and grandson, who love me unconditionally.

First, Some Context

In my 20-year leadership career, I have seen managers and supervisors struggle in holding their employees accountable. This has been true for many people in supervisory roles and with various levels of authority and experience, from newly minted, first-time supervisors to seasoned managers responsible for entire workforces. What has stood out to me is the lack of balance in their performance management approach. Managers and supervisors who have struggled to hold their employees accountable and improve performance the right way have either been too harsh, too lenient, or too disengaged. These approaches have been detrimental.

In this book, I unveil Supportive Accountability Leadership™, a simple yet powerful framework that will help you create a positive work environment while improving performance. I developed this model based on two decades of my personal experience. According to peer-reviewed international research in various disciplines, leaders can successfully apply the seven elements of the model to improve performance for individuals, teams, and entire workforces.

To provide you with examples of how to apply the performance management principles in this book, I tell the story of Vic, Alex, and Mary of YouthZone, a nonprofit organization, as well as other stories. These stories were inspired by real-life experiences in my leadership career; however, all the characters, organizations, and events are fictitious. Any resemblance to real people, events, organizations, or programs is merely coincidental and unintentional.

The story of Vic and Mary provides examples of data, reports, forms, and other tools. These are for illustration purposes only. You have permission to use any of the sample templates and customize them to meet your needs.

While this book provides a solid foundation and starting point for effective employee performance management, results can't be guaranteed, and success depends on the specifics of your unique situation. As you apply the concepts and tools in this book, seek the guidance of your organization's designated performance management and legal experts. They can help you minimize risk to you and your organization.

Although I am a management consultant, the purchase of this book doesn't establish a consulting relationship between us. If you're interested in learning more about my company's consulting and training services, please email me at smelena@melenaconsulting.com or visit my website at www.LeadershipStrength.com.

Thank you, and enjoy the book!
Sylvia Melena

Contents

Introduction

Y ou landed a job supervising employees. When you took the job, you were full of passion and energy and ready to take on the world. Then the inevitable happened. You're faced with an employee who has significant performance issues that seem insurmountable. You completed extensive supervisor training and collected a wealth of information about employee performance management, but it hasn't worked. You're frustrated, overwhelmed, and drained.

You're not alone. I have seen hundreds of leaders go through the angst of trying to work with struggling employees. In the last 14 years, I have taught and coached managers and supervisors to help underperforming employees and document quickly and efficiently. The goal has always been success, not to "get rid" of people.

My name is Sylvia Melena, and I am the Founder and CEO of Melena Consulting Group, a leadership and management consulting and training company based in San Diego County, California. I have a Master's in Leadership and Organizational Studies and experience in middle, senior, and executive management. Most importantly, I have a passion for leadership and a profound love for people. It's out of this background that I developed the Supportive Accountability Leadership™ Model, which provides leaders with a balanced approach to performance management.

The Supportive Accountability Leadership™ Model

Supportive Accountability Leadership™ is a simple yet powerful framework that will help you engage employees and improve performance. At the core of the model is supportive accountability, a blend of supportive supervision and strong accountability that sparks employee performance.

With supportive accountability, you can achieve one of three outcomes:

Outcome #1 - You can help the employee turn around substandard performance and achieve success. This is the ultimate goal of Supportive Accountability Leadership and the most rewarding of the three outcomes.

Outcome #2 - The employee discovers that the job isn't a good fit and embraces a new role where he or she can succeed. This is a "win-win-win" for you, the employee, and your organization.

Outcome #3 - The employee continues to underperform and is removed from the position. This isn't the goal, but it's sometimes necessary so that you, your team, and your organization can achieve success. And success is about the people you were hired to serve—employees, customers, and the leadership of your organization.

If you're uncomfortable with outcome number three, you're not alone. Many supervisors struggle with disciplinary action. Let's face it. Discipline isn't the fun part of our jobs as leaders. However, when you chose to become a leader, it became an essential part of your role. It's a necessary element of effective performance management.

The Four Leadership Styles of Supportive Accountability™

Supportive Accountability Leadership frames performance management using four basic leadership styles. These styles are determined by how much leaders strike a delicate balance between supportiveness and accountability. In this book, I will provide a brief overview of these four leadership styles—supportive unaccountability, unsupportive accountability, total avoidance, and supportive accountability. However, our focus throughout the book will be solely on supportive accountability and how you can use this balanced leadership approach to engage employees and promote strong performance.

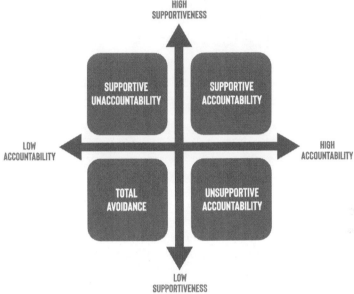

FOUR LEADERSHIP STYLES OF SUPPORTIVE ACCOUNTABILITY™

HIGH SUPPORTIVENESS

SUPPORTIVE UNACCOUNTABILITY

SUPPORTIVE ACCOUNTABILITY

LOW ACCOUNTABILITY

HIGH ACCOUNTABILITY

TOTAL AVOIDANCE

UNSUPPORTIVE ACCOUNTABILITY

LOW SUPPORTIVENESS

Seven Elements of Effective Performance Management

The Supportive Accountability Leadership Model will also help you navigate the employee performance management process using the seven elements of effective performance management: expectations, monitoring, feedback, support, recognition, accountability, and documentation. I will show you how to use these elements to ignite performance for all employees, not just for those who are struggling. Effective performance management is for all employees and keeps your organization at the top of its game.

DOCUMENTATION EXPECTATIONS

ACCOUNTABILITY SUPPORTIVE ACCOUNTABILITY MONITORING

RECOGNITION FEEDBACK

SUPPORT

SUPPORTIVE ACCOUNTABILITY LEADERSHIP™

Progressive Discipline Basics

To help you with employees who continue to struggle, even with a significant investment of your time, energy, and support, I will cover the basics of progressive discipline.

If you're looking for a cookie-cutter approach to progressive discipline, there is none. Effective progressive discipline requires skill, sound judgment, and the support of your direct manager and human resources experts. I will show you how to do that. I will provide you an overview of progressive discipline, the levels involved, and how the process works. Each organization has its specific policies, procedures, and philosophy regarding progressive discipline. It's vital that you consult with key people to ensure you're in alignment with your organization's protocols.

Documentation Made Easier

And then there's that dreaded documentation. It's draining and time-consuming, but necessary. I will show you how to lighten the burden of documenting performance. This book provides documentation examples, tips, and templates that you can use as is or customize to meet your needs. It also includes a free download of the Performance Documentation Toolkit. To bring it all together, I have also dedicated an entire chapter to best practices in documentation. However, these resources will never trump the guidance you must seek from your organization's designated experts.

A Strong Supervisor-Employee Relationship

In the bigger scheme of things, none of this matters if you don't focus your energies on the most crucial factor for unleashing performance excellence: a strong supervisor-employee relationship. A solid and healthy supervisor-employee relationship is the foundation of the Supportive Accountability Leadership Model. All the rest will be to no avail if you don't get this right. As the immediate supervisor, you alone can break or make the workplace in the eyes of employees. So this entire book, from the first chapter to the last, focuses on how you can be a great supervisor. I will unveil the art of supportive leadership to help you unleash the potential of the people you lead.

Supportive Accountability Leadership isn't just for turning around substandard performance. It's the bedrock of performance excellence. It can also help employees who are doing well to take their performance to higher levels. So whether you want to jump-start performance for your new employees, transform good performance into performance excellence, or turn around lackluster performance, Supportive Accountability Leadership will provide you a firm foundation for immediate and long-lasting success.

Chapter 1
The Heart of Supportive Accountability

*"We just have to create a work environment where whatever is going on
with our team, we let them know that there is somebody there."*

– Scott H. Silverman, CEO of Confidential Recovery

In my 20-year leadership career, I have seen managers and supervisors struggle in holding their employees accountable. This has been true for numerous people in supervisory roles and with various levels of authority and experience, from newly minted, first-time supervisors to seasoned managers responsible for entire workforces. What has stood out to me is the lack of balance in their performance management process. Managers and supervisors who have struggled to hold their employees accountable and improve performance the right way have either been too harsh, too lenient, or too disengaged.

These three extreme and unbalanced approaches are ineffective and negatively impact the workplace. The key to effective performance management is to strike a delicate balance between two different yet complementary performance management elements—supportiveness and accountability. This balance is the core principle that makes the Supportive Accountability Leadership Model so effective.

The Four Leadership Styles of Supportive Accountability™

The Supportive Accountability Leadership Model frames performance management using four basic leadership styles determined by how much leaders strike a delicate balance between support and accountability. These four styles are depicted below based on high and low levels of supportiveness and accountability.

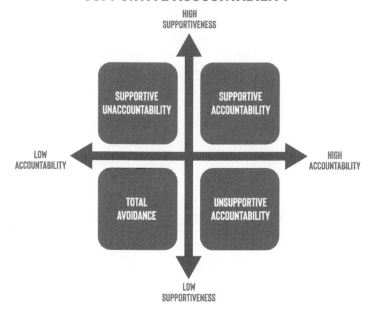

Leaders can operate anywhere in the continuum between high and low for both supportiveness and accountability, and the amount of support and accountability required will vary from situation to situation.

1. ***Unsupportive Accountability*** is characterized by high levels of accountability and low levels of supportiveness. Leaders with this style demand high performance but don't provide the necessary tools, equipment, and emotional support employees need to achieve it. This type of accountability can create a harsh, intimidating, and uncaring environment for employees. Leaders who use an unsupportive accountability style pile on the work with minimal support and create

a demanding work environment. They're often successful in pressuring employees to deliver high performance, but at extraordinary costs to employees and the organization.

2. ***Supportive Unaccountability*** is demonstrated by high levels of supportiveness and low levels of accountability. Leaders who operate with a high degree of supportive unaccountability tend to worry too much about being liked and making employees happy. They have difficulty holding themselves and their employees accountable for meeting organizational goals and priorities. They create a fun environment but struggle to help employees meet expectations. Supportive unaccountability can create a "feel-good" atmosphere on the surface, but it doesn't promote employee engagement and workplace fairness. While some employees are self-motivated and will achieve excellence with or without adequate accountability, there are others who need the oversight to meet performance standards. When a leader fails to promote accountability, it results in an environment where not everyone carries their weight, which sinks the morale of high-performing employees.

3. ***Total Avoidance*** is the absence of both supportiveness and accountability. This is a hands-off approach, where leaders relinquish their responsibility to lead, guide, inspire, and hold themselves and their employees accountable for meeting goals. Leaders who display total avoidance don't address concerns, which causes them to snowball into bigger issues that require a higher degree of intervention down the line. Leaders who approach performance management with total avoidance don't actually "manage" performance. Instead of getting ahead of problems, they operate in a reactive mode and only spring into action when fires erupt. You can spot these leaders frequently expending their energies handling unnecessary "emergencies." The total avoidance approach creates a chaotic

work environment and causes unnecessary workplace stress for the leaders and the people they lead. When leaders who operate with total avoidance oversee an entire workforce, it creates significant organizational dysfunction.

4. ***Supportive Accountability*** is the most effective performance management style. It embodies a high level of supportiveness complemented by a high level of accountability. There's no magic formula for how much support and accountability are needed. Effective leaders provide the right amount of support and accountability based on each situation. When performance isn't quite up to par, they don't look for a person to blame, but rather seek to uncover the underlying causes and to provide the support necessary for success. They ask themselves how they can improve the way they lead, provide support, and promote accountability. Leaders who manage with supportive accountability know that great performance flows out of a strong supervisor-employee relationship based on mutual trust, caring, and respect.

The Supervisor-Employee Relationship

The supervisor-employee relationship is the foundation of Supportive Accountability Leadership. If you're going to inspire employees to achieve success, you must first and foremost build a lasting and healthy working relationship with each of them. To accomplish this, get to know each employee on a professional and personal level. You don't need to know their innermost secrets, but rather to understand and appreciate their needs, priorities, desires, aspirations, strengths, weaknesses, and fears. The more you know about each employee, the more you can create a great work environment where people can thrive.

Seven Elements of Effective Performance Management

Supportive Accountability Leadership encompasses seven elements of effective performance management: expectations, monitoring, feedback, support, recognition, accountability, and documentation. These elements are not necessarily sequential and are all interconnected. Effective leaders are agile and use the elements that each situation requires. In the chapters that follow, we will explore each of these and how to implement them in the spirit of supportive accountability.

SUPPORTIVE ACCOUNTABILITY
LEADERSHIP™

Supportive Accountability Is a Choice

The Four Leadership Styles of Supportive Accountability are not about personality. They're about the approach. For instance, you may have a direct, take-charge personality and yet choose to provide support and accountability with grace, humility, respect, and sincere regard for the feelings and well-being of others. Likewise, you may be a soft-spoken, gentle person and still demonstrate a respectful firmness when holding yourself and employees accountable. Whatever your personality, you can intentionally choose your leadership style. This is one of the most important choices you will make as a leader, and it will have a profound impact on the success and well-being of the people you lead. It will also influence your ability to recruit and retain top talent, which will affect your overall performance and that of your organization.

The intent of the four leadership styles isn't to label you, but rather to provide a framework to help you discover your performance management approach. This discovery is merely a starting point on your journey towards supportive accountability and performance management excellence. Supportive Accountability Leadership can be learned. However, before the learning process can begin, you must understand where you are today and decide where you want to be tomorrow.

In Review

The key takeaway is that strong leadership is paramount for creating an environment that engages employees and promotes strong performance. Leaders who are proactive and balanced in their leadership approach engage employees and create a motivating work environment. Leaders who are too harsh or too lenient or who avoid their responsibilities altogether create a disengaging work environment. This leads to less-than-optimum performance. The great news is that capable leadership is a skill that can be learned and refined over time. Managers and supervisors can enhance their ability to develop, support, and hold employees accountable and create a motivating and high-performing work environment.

Putting It into Action

1. Review the descriptions of the four leadership styles of supportive accountability—unsupportive accountability, supportive unaccountability, total avoidance, and supportive accountability.

2. Self-reflect. In which style do you most consistently operate? Are you high or low in accountability? Are you high or low in supportiveness?

3. Keep this self-reflection in mind as you read more about support and accountability in the rest of this book and write down ways you can improve in supportiveness, accountability, or both.

Chapter 2
The Art of Supportive Leadership

*A strong supervisor-employee relationship is the most important source
of support you can provide employees.*

Leaders who effectively identify and meet the support needs of
employees are in a much better position to unleash employee
potential and boost workplace performance. In the Supportive
Accountability Leadership Model, support is anything the employee
reasonably needs to achieve strong job performance. An employee
won't be able to succeed and sustain success over time without
adequate support.

SUPPORTIVE ACCOUNTABILITY
LEADERSHIP™

Support fosters a work environment where the employee can thrive. As a supervisor, you're the most important source of support for employees, and this support starts with a strong supervisor-employee relationship.

The Supervisor-Employee Relationship

You're the "face" of the organization. Everything you do and say represents the organization in the eyes of its employees.[1] How you interact with people on a daily basis will affect their perception of the leadership, supportiveness, and fairness of both you and your organization. This perception of fairness affects how much employees will trust you and your organization.

You have substantial influence, and this influence impacts the quality of the workplace and the success of your organization. This requires that you bring your best to work every day. Research has consistently shown that the supervisor-employee relationship influences employee perception of support, engagement, commitment to the organization, turnover intentions, ethical behavior, and ultimately performance.[2] You, much more than any other workplace factor, impact employees' decision to stay with or leave your organization. The quality of your relationships with employees affects their perception of organizational support. And these perceptions affect retention.[3]

Many Employees Don't Feel Supported

The sad truth is that many employees don't feel empowered or supported in their workplaces. Surveys of employees in the U.S. have consistently shown that most view their supervisor as the greatest source of workplace stress.[4] Supervisors are a chief contributor to employee burnout.[5] This underscores the vital role that you as a leader play in creating a supportive and empowering work environment that can retain top talent, keep employees healthy, and promote the success of your organization. The way you approach employee performance management can either increase or reduce stress and burnout for employees.

Vic's Top Priority

It was a beautiful morning in May. The five supervisors of the Youth Employment Program's leadership team cheered as the manager shared the program's performance data for April. Among the supervisors present in YouthZone's conference room, Vic was especially proud. For the second month in a row, his unit of seven youth employment specialists had earned him recognition as the top-performing supervisor in the Youth Employment Program. Being the best in the small nonprofit's employment program for low-income youth energized him. It's what he lived for.

Vic was enjoying the applause when the receptionist interrupted the meeting.

"Excuse me," she said. The applause came to a sudden halt, and all heads turned as she walked over to Vic and handed him a note. "There's a teenager in the lobby, and he wants to talk to you. I told him you're in a meeting, but he's insisting on seeing you right away."

By now, all eyes were on Vic, and he could feel them.

"Okay," he said as he took the note. "I'll be right there." He could feel the heat rising in his face. He turned towards his manager and his peers, who were all still looking at him in awkward silence. "I'm sorry," he said, waving the note in his hand. "I have to see this customer."

As he sped out of the conference room, thoughts ran through his head. *I can't believe it. It better not be about Mary again. If I get one more complaint!*

"Excuse me. Are you Mary's supervisor?" A young man broke into his thoughts.

"Yes." Vic composed himself. "My name is Vic. I'm Mary's supervisor. How may I help you?"

Indeed, it was another complaint about Mary's customer service. This was the third time this month. But in his usual charming manner, Vic handled it. The young man complained about Mary's rudeness. Vic appeased him. And that was that.

Vic had better things to do. After all, great team performance doesn't happen by itself. If he was going to be promoted, he needed to be the best. As long as he could keep the complaints from reaching his manager, everything was under control.

Three Pillars of a Strong Supervisor-Employee Relationship

The three pillars of a strong supervisor-employee relationship are trust, effective communication, and empowerment. When you consistently live by these three pillars, you establish a relationship that's rewarding for you and the employee.

The First Pillar: Trust

Trust is the foundation for all healthy relationships, and the supervisor-employee relationship is no exception.

As such, trust fosters strong teamwork, cooperation, information sharing, problem-solving, and conflict resolution. A high degree of workplace trust drives higher levels of employee diligence, productivity, and innovation. These lead to stronger organizational performance.[6]

Employees trust you as a leader when they believe your intentions towards them are good and they feel safe being vulnerable with you.[7] The way you interact with the people you serve will have a direct impact on how much they will trust you and your organization. Employees trust leaders who care about them, demonstrate honesty, create a safe environment, act in fairness and consistency, and keep their promises.

Caring. People matter above all else. Leaders who care about people have a positive impact on performance.[8] They care about employees. They care about customers. And they care about their leaders. Don't sacrifice the health, safety, and well-being of people to meet performance goals.

Employees are people, not merely human resources, assets, or capital. They're someone's mother, father, son, daughter, spouse, friend, or neighbor. They show up to work every day with their needs, priorities, hopes, dreams, fears, and concerns. To genuinely care about people, you must first get to know them. This doesn't mean that you pry into their personal lives, but rather that you listen carefully. You would be surprised how much you can learn about what makes people tick if you simply listen. The more you know about people, the more you can support them and the more they know you care.

Honesty. Trust requires honesty. Share the bigger picture regarding goals, objectives, and pressing matters, and people will go the extra mile for you. When people ask you a question that you can't answer because of confidentiality, laws, or ethical reasons, say so. Employees will value and appreciate your honesty.

Where there's honesty, there's no room for manipulation or hidden agendas. Employees know when leaders are dishonest. If you use deceit or manipulation to get things done, it may work for a while, but sooner or later people will figure it out. When the moment of truth comes, your credibility will be damaged, and this will hamper your effectiveness.

Safety. Create an environment where people feel safe being honest and vulnerable with you. When you create a safe environment, employees will be open with you. They will let you know about their needs, struggles, and concerns without fear of reprisal. They will feel free to express their thoughts honestly, even when their perspectives differ from yours. Don't use this vulnerability against them, but rather to understand how you can best support them and help them achieve success. When employees know you have their backs, they will have yours.

Fairness. Treat everyone fairly. Let fairness and justice be the hallmark of how you rate performance, distribute resources, provide rewards, and select people for choice assignments. Have an objective and standardized decision-making system and adhere to it. Be transparent about your system and let employees know what it takes to reap the rewards. Employees shouldn't have to guess what it takes to earn excellent performance ratings, receive recognition, or cash in on other perks.

Consistency. Be consistent in what you say and do. You can't show compassion one moment and lash out the next. People need predictability. Employees can't feel safe if they don't know what to expect from you. They will be uneasy approaching you if they can't anticipate how you will react. Uncertainty creates a stressful environment, and this stress is detrimental to employees' health and success and to that of your organization.

Promise Keeping. Keep your promises. Be careful with what you say and how you say it, as promises can be made directly or merely implied. Once you commit, employees expect you to deliver. Failure to follow through will damage trust.

Trust takes effort to build and sustain over time and can be quickly lost. Once trust is lost, it takes a tremendous amount of work to repair the damage and earn it back. The great news is that when trust has been firmly established and your supervisor-employee relationship is rock solid, employees will be more forgiving and understanding when you make mistakes. Each interaction you have with employees is a golden opportunity to earn and reinforce trust. Use these opportunities to build strong supervisor-employee relationships that lead to success and create a thriving workplace.

The Second Pillar: Effective Communication

Effective communication fosters a cooperative working relationship where you and the employee exchange information, resources, and support. Effective communication is frequent, high-quality, two-way, collaborative, and individualized.

Frequent and High-Quality. High-quality communication is marked by mutual respect, caring, concern, and collaboration.[9] With all the competing priorities you face every day, it's easy to become bogged down with administrative tasks. And while you can't completely sacrifice the administrative aspect of your work for the sake of frequent, high-quality communication, you do need to achieve and maintain balance.

Frequent, high-quality communication doesn't have to be formal or require a great deal of documentation. It's best to use a variety of methods to communicate with employees in group and individual settings. When you invest time and energy into strengthening your communication, you and employees will reap the rewards of a strong supervisor-employee relationship.

Two-Way. High-quality communication requires a reciprocal, two-way exchange of information.[10] You can't have an adequate exchange of information if you're doing all the talking. Listen more and talk less to gain a deeper understanding of each employee's needs, priorities, hopes, dreams, fears, and concerns. This deeper understanding is essential to building mutual trust and respect. Two-way communication allows employees to clarify questions, squelch rumors, and understand your overarching vision and that of your organization. It helps them feel empowered and develop a positive perception of the workplace.

Collaborative. Facilitate collaborative conversations. Tap into the rich talent, experience, and diversity of employees in the decision-making process. Engage their ideas, thoughts, and perspectives. Don't shy away from healthy disagreement, but rather embrace it as an opportunity to scrutinize issues and make decisions as a team. Allow room for negotiation and discussion, both in group and one-on-one settings. This will go a long way towards building and reinforcing trust. It may be tempting to pull rank as a leader and order employees to do things because you say so. However, please understand that if you rule as a dictator, you will foster fear, discontent, disengagement, anger, or other negative emotions. Such an environment isn't sustainable. Something will eventually give. Depending on the severity of the situation, the consequences could be employee burnout, high turnover, sabotage, or even uprising.

Individualized. We all have different communication styles and preferences. Individualized communication respects, appreciates, and unleashes the power of these differences to spark ideas and innovation. No communication style is better than another, and all communication styles have their peaks and valleys. Peaks are when our communication styles and differences help us achieve positive results. Valleys are when our communication styles and differences create unhealthy conflict and undermine teamwork and collaboration.

Each communication style serves an important purpose on the team. However, we can experience challenges when we communicate with others whose styles are different than ours. As leaders, we can experience frustration and misunderstandings in the supervisor-employee relationship when our communication approaches and preferences clash with those of our direct reports. Since we walk in our own skin, it's easy to view our communication approach as superior and to expect others to change their styles to accommodate ours. I have been guilty of this myself and, when I am not careful, can continue to be. I must continually remind myself to adapt my communication approach to meet the needs of others.

Adapting our styles to meet the needs of others doesn't imply that we must tolerate blatantly disrespectful communication, such as the use of profanity, yelling, name-calling, and the like. Not addressing unacceptable communication will create a toxic work environment.

As a leader, focus on your communication preferences and on those of the people you lead. There are assessments, training, and resources on the market that can help you understand communication styles and differences and how you can capitalize on them to promote collaboration and achieve positive results. These tools can help you navigate the complexities of the various communication styles. They also provide a common point of reference for team communication.

When we adapt effectively, we help employees feel cared about, safe, and secure. We inspire trust and position ourselves to provide the best support possible for them to succeed.

The Third Pillar: Empowerment

Empowerment is the process by which leaders give employees the power and authority to make decisions at their level, recognize and solve problems,[11] and go above and beyond expectations. In an article published by the *American Journal of Economics and Business Administration,* J.D. Tony Carter asserted that "the key goal for managers is to understand the balance of performance elements… and trust their employees by empowering them to help the organization."[12]

Empowerment promotes employee satisfaction[13] and strong performance.[14] It motivates employees to be innovative and to champion organizational excellence. True empowerment creates a safe environment for employees to look beyond the status quo and respectfully challenge their leadership's thinking. Leaders who are secure in themselves welcome and even crave this type of healthy debate. They know it encourages diverse perspectives and sparks innovation, leading to more efficient ways of doing business. Empowerment gives employees the freedom, trust, and self-confidence to identify their own support needs and share these needs with their leaders.

Involve Employees. To be an empowering leader, you must first come to grips with the fact that you don't have all the answers no matter how brilliant, educated, or experienced you are. Intentionally encourage employees to bring their thinking caps to work and involve them in the decision-making process when appropriate and feasible. Promote healthy team debate around decisions, issues, ideas, and other work-related topics to consider pros, cons, and major pitfalls. This is the complete opposite of establishing a culture of "yes" people. To be an empowering leader, don't just encourage but expect employees to add value to the organization by sharing their ideas and opinions. Create an environment where employees feel compelled to openly share what they really think, not what the powers that be expect them to say.

Actively pursue employee input on a continuous basis. Having an "open door" policy where employees are free to come to your office is good, but it doesn't promote candid input from those who are too shy or intimidated to visit you. Proactively ask employees what they think and encourage their honesty. When they answer with candor, listen, suspend judgment, and think before you react and respond. You're not expected to be completely immune from negative emotions when criticism comes your way. However, people expect you to maintain professionalism and composure and to try to understand their perspectives. As the leader, you set the tone for communication in the workplace. You also bear the responsibility for creating an environment of supportive accountability and collaborative problem-solving.

Abandon Micromanagement. Trust employees to get the job done. Great leaders don't give employees a play-by-play on how they need to arrive at their goals. Of course, employees will need to comply with established processes, rules, regulations, guidelines, and ethical standards. However, barring these constraints, great leaders give employees the freedom to approach their work in a manner that works for them.

Everyone has differences in work styles, talents, and preferences. Empowerment respects these differences and focuses on results. Clarify the expected results, develop employees, and give them the autonomy to get the job done in a way that works for them. Check in with them from time to time to ensure things are going in the right direction and to provide them with the necessary support, but give them, and yourself, the freedom to succeed.

Strike a Balance. While empowerment is a vital support element that promotes strong organizational performance, we must not confuse it with a "free-for-all" where there's a complete absence of support and accountability. A "free-for-all" is a leadership style of total avoidance.

Managers and supervisors must be skilled at achieving a balance between empowerment and accountability. While empowerment allows employees to make decisions at their level, accountability provides them with the appropriate framework for making these decisions within the expectations, values, and scope defined by the organization. To expect employees to work autonomously and make decisions without providing a solid foundation isn't empowering.

Determine Employee Readiness. To provide the appropriate amount of autonomy, gauge each employee's experience, skill level, talent, and the task at hand. For instance, if the employee is new to the role, this is the first time the employee will perform the work or project, or the employee is having performance difficulties, you may need to provide more detailed instructions and guidance for her to be successful. The same is true if the task is highly technical or requires a specific set of steps or procedures. On the other hand, if you're working with a seasoned, high-performing employee who is already familiar with the task and prefers independence, get out of the way. In any case, provide as much autonomy as appropriate and feasible given the specific situation and the individual employee's needs and preferences.

Develop Employees. As a leader, you have a responsibility to adequately prepare and develop employees to operate in an empowering environment. You can use a variety of practices to build employee capacity for more autonomy, decision-making, and involvement. These may include clear communication, coaching, employee participation, training programs, rewards,[15] new-employee onboarding, mentoring programs, progressive levels of responsibility, and stretch assignments. These practices equip employees to understand the priorities of the organization, know their jobs well, and make sound decisions.

Unleash Performance. Research has demonstrated that empowerment promotes employee trust, which increases employee engagement and translates to strong employee performance.[16] Several decades of research have also revealed that empowerment has a positive effect on employee satisfaction and commitment to the organization.[17] This isn't surprising. Employees are happiest when working in empowering, collaborative environments because they're conducive to team cohesion, information sharing, and openness to various perspectives and ideas.

Promote Customer Service Excellence. Empowered employees are in a better position to provide excellent customer service. Empowerment allows employees to make decisions quickly, without having to go through lengthy decision-making channels. In a culture of empowerment, employees who work directly with customers can tailor their service immediately, without having to go through layers of approval.[18] They can do this because their management has created an environment where they're free and safe to make decisions. Thus, empowerment creates efficiency. It also motivates and equips employees to deliver fast and responsive service that promotes a highly satisfying customer experience.

Start at the Top. Supportive leadership is paramount in creating a culture of empowerment. When managers and supervisors collectively create a supportive and empowering work environment, employees feel freedom and control over their daily work.[19] Leaders who routinely manage with high command and control leadership styles disempower employees and cause a high degree of interpersonal conflict.[20]

An environment of empowerment increases employee morale, creativity,[21] and productivity.[22] In this type of environment, employees are committed to going above and beyond the call of duty to ensure the success of fellow employees[23] and the organization.

In Review

A strong supervisor-employee relationship is the most important source of support you can provide employees. Your ability to deliver other types of support hinges on the caliber of your professional relationship with employees. If you want to create a workplace that inspires employees to deliver results, building a strong supervisor-employee relationship through supportive accountability is paramount.

To unleash employee potential and boost workplace performance, you must become well versed in the art of supportive leadership. Employees can't succeed and sustain success without adequate support. How well you can identify and meet the support needs of the people you supervise will hinge on the quality of the relationships you build. You can enhance these relationships with the three pillars of a strong supervisor-employee relationship—trust, effective communication, and empowerment. When you successfully apply these three pillars, you foster relationships that are rewarding and engaging, and that promote strong performance.

Putting It into Action

Strengthen your relationship with your direct reports using the three pillars of a strong supervisor-employee relationship—trust, effective communication, and empowerment.

1. Build Trust: Get to know employees as individuals so you can genuinely care about them and support them. Talk to them. Find out what is important to each of them. Is it family, pets, hobbies, or something else? Listen and take note.

2. Promote Effective Communication: Assess your communication style and preferences, as well as those of individual employees. Consider using one of the many assessments, training, and tools available to enhance workplace communication.

3. Increase Empowerment: Involve employees. Seek their ideas, suggestions, and opinions.

    ◦ Implement a suggestion box and act on the suggestions.

    ◦ Schedule a team decision-making meeting the next time you need to solve a problem, implement a change, or start a new project.

    ◦ If you manage a large office or department, host an open forum for all employees.

Chapter 3
Expectations that Inspire

Helping employees understand the humanity of what they do every day makes the goals established for them much more meaningful.

Expectations are the beginning of great performance and the foundation for achieving success. They tell employees what they're aiming for. Expectations that inspire provide the bigger picture of why their work is important, what they need to achieve, and how their achievements will be measured. Without a clear understanding of what is expected of them, employees will be aiming in the dark, not knowing where they're headed or the ultimate purpose of their work.

SUPPORTIVE ACCOUNTABILITY LEADERSHIP™

The Reality Check

Victor was sitting in his office, reviewing the Youth Employment Program's daily performance report. The program was doing well, but his unit was knocking it out of the ballpark. Vic smiled. His team was definitely in the running for first place again. This would be the third month in a row. If he could keep this up, he would be next in line for a promotion to management.

The phone rang. "Hello," Vic answered. "Yes, I'll be right there."

He hung up the phone, grabbed a pen and paper, and dashed to his manager's office. The door was open, so he walked in. "Hi, Alex."

Alexandra looked up from her desk, holding a paper in her hand as Vic approached. "Hi, Vic. Please have a seat," she said. Vic sat down in the chair in front of Alex's desk.

"I got a complaint about Mary," Alex said as she handed Vic a handwritten letter. "Please take a look."

Vic read the letter. The contents were not surprising. *Dear Manager, I was in the office today to see my counselor, Mary. I asked her to help me fill out a job application, but she was really rude. She wouldn't help me and said I should have paid attention in the job application class. I tried to tell her why I needed help, but she wouldn't listen. She just kept talking. I'm so frustrated. I can't work with her anymore, but I really need a job. Please help me and give me another counselor.* The letter ended with a teen girl's name and phone number.

Vic looked up at Alex after reading the letter. "I'll call the customer right away."

"No need to," Alex responded. "I already did. The letter was addressed to me and I wanted to hear for myself. If this is true, it's unacceptable. Mary's job is to help our youths find jobs. Our youths are vulnerable and many of them are struggling to make ends meet.

They come here for hope, to get help, to learn new skills. Not to be belittled."

"I agree," Vic said.

Alex continued. "The interesting thing is that this young lady said she talked to you twice last month about similar incidents with Mary. Is this true?"

"Yes," Vic answered. "But…" Then silence.

"What did she say?" Alex asked.

Vic grabbed his collar and took a deep breath. He recounted the two previous complaints from this particular girl as best he could. He remembered some of it because the incidents were recent, but the details were fuzzy. By now, his palms were sweaty and the room felt stuffy. Alex just listened as Vic spoke, but her serious face said it all.

When Vic was done, Alex asked, "Why didn't you let me know about these two previous incidents?"

"I didn't want to bother you," Vic replied. "You're really busy. You have so much going on, so I handled them myself."

"How did you handle them?" Alex inquired.

Vic hesitated for a split second. "I, uh… I called the customer and resolved the issue. Both times she just needed a little guidance, and I provided it to her."

"Did you talk to Mary about these two prior incidents?" Alex continued to probe.

"No. I didn't talk to her," Vic answered.

"Look," Alex said, "at this point, you can't go back and fix how you handled these two incidents with Mary. But I do want to clarify what I expect from you going forward and how we're going to address this latest incident."

Alex jotted a couple of notes in her notebook and continued. "First of all, whenever you get any type of complaint—written, in person, on the phone—it doesn't matter how you get it, you're going to come and see me right away to let me know. And the two of us are going to discuss it and agree on how you're going to handle it. I need to be kept informed of all complaints you receive, not just Mary's. No matter how large or small, I need to know."

Vic nodded his head.

"Now, is there anything else I need to know? Anything else you didn't tell me about?"

Vic thoughts raced through his head. *Should I tell Alex about Mary's other complaints? She said she wants to know. But there were so many, and Alex isn't going to be happy. Besides, I can't even remember them all. No, I won't tell her. I'll just start fresh. Yes, I'll just start fresh.*

"Vic?" Alex pressed him for an answer.

"No, we're good to go."

Alex continued, "Now about this latest complaint…"

Alex and Vic discussed at length the approach Vic would take to address this last complaint with Mary.

Using Goals to Inspire

To promote great performance, it's not enough to establish expectations. You must inspire. People are born for greatness. Deep down inside of us, there's a yearning to make a difference in this world. When our last day on this earth comes to an end, we want our lives to have mattered. We want to have accomplished something significant or to have made this world a better place. We desire a life with meaning. Some people are more aware of this desire than others. This craving for meaning is a big motivator, both at home and in the workplace.

Painting the Vision

As a leader, you must create a sense of meaning in the workplace. You must paint a vivid picture of why the work that you and your employees do matters and how it makes a difference. At the center of this picture, you must place the vision of your organization and how it makes a difference. If you don't believe in your organization's vision or your values are not aligned with the vision, you won't be able to inspire employees to advance it. You must either come into alignment with what your organization is trying to accomplish or explore your options.

Effective goals advance your organization's vision. Continuously communicate your organization's vision and how achieving established performance goals will advance it. It's the vision, not the number of widgets you produce or the number of contacts you make, that will inspire those around you and ignite employee passion to deliver excellence. Goals that focus solely on money, production levels, or other mundane measurements don't inspire. To inspire employees, intentionally make the connection between your organization's measurable goals and how they promote the organization's greater good and bring out the best in humanity.

To unleash the passion within employees and see performance soar, you must humanize your organization's goals and articulate the deeper meaning of their impact. When you humanize goals, you're no longer focusing on quality assurance goals for the production of airplane parts; you're promoting the safety of the men, women, and children who fly on the airplanes comprised of these parts. You're not merely complying with food service regulations, but preventing foodborne illnesses and keeping your community safe. You're not merely processing applications for social services programs; you're providing the vital services that people need to lead healthy, safe, and productive lives. Helping employees understand the humanity of what they do every day makes the goals established for them much more meaningful.

Share the vision and the associated goals far and wide: at staff meetings and unit meetings, in newsletters and electronic messaging boards, and at every opportunity you can think of. Keeping the vision alive creates and maintains a sense of meaning. Without these constant reminders of why their work matters, people can become complacent, work can become a daily grind, and employee passion for the organization's greater good can be extinguished.

YouthZone's Vision

YouthZone was a community-based organization that provided various types of educational and employment programs for low-income youth. YouthZone's vision was "to empower youth through education and employment to live healthy, safe, and productive lives and reach their full potential." This vision was YouthZone's greater good and what made the work of its employees meaningful.

As the program manager of the Youth Employment Program, Alex was passionate about this vision. She understood well the struggles of the hundreds of young people served by YouthZone. She had grown up in a low-income community facing what often felt like insurmountable odds to succeed. She had been fortunate enough to cross paths with people who believed in her and helped her when she needed it the most. But Alex knew that not every youth had someone to turn to. This was why the work of YouthZone was so important to her, and she was committed to seeing it through. She expected her staff to deliver prompt and efficient service and to treat the youths with the utmost respect. Excellent customer service wasn't optional. It was an expectation.

Using Goals for Employee Self-Development

Decades of research have demonstrated a positive link between performance goals and job performance. Van Yperen, Blaga & Postmes conducted a meta-analysis of 98 papers published through January 1, 2015, involving 33,983 participants. Let's review the researchers' findings regarding two types of goals, which we will refer to as self-development goals and peer comparison goals.[24]

Self-Development Goals

Self-development goals focus employees on their own development. Supervisors evaluate performance based on how well employees have mastered a task or a project compared to established expectations and standards. There's a strong link between self-development goals and job performance, both in employees' regular duties and in tasks beyond their roles. People who focus on self-development and mastery of their jobs, instead of on outperforming others, develop healthier work habits. They demonstrate an interest in their work, cooperation, and drive to achieve performance excellence. They respect different perspectives and opinions and share resources.[25] This promotes a healthy and cooperative work environment.

Peer Comparison Goals

Peer comparison goals base employees' success on how their performance compares to that of other employees.[26] Evaluating employee performance in comparison to their peers can promote increased effort to meet goals and result in high performance, but it can also have negative side effects on employees. Research has revealed several pros and cons when it comes to using peer comparison goals. On the one hand, striving to perform better than others can lead to a positive learning experience, promote increased employee effort, stimulate a "need for achievement," build employee self-confidence, generate quality work, motivate employees to aim higher, and ultimately improve performance.[27]

On the other hand, peer comparison goals can be detrimental. They can produce "anxiety, worry, negative affect (negative emotions), dissatisfaction, and strained interpersonal relationships." They can demotivate, increase dysfunctional perfectionism, and threaten employees since failure to perform may demonstrate a "lack of ability in comparison to others." Evaluating individuals who are not performance-oriented in comparison to others can be especially harmful.[28]

A Balanced Approach

The key to establishing healthy performance goals is to strike a balance between self-development goals and peer comparison goals.

Don't compare employees to others when establishing goals, evaluating performance, and providing feedback. Focus them on meeting established standards. This approach creates a less stressful and more comfortable working environment.[29] It promotes accountability but focuses on the employee's self-development and improvement. The employee's success is based on a fixed target—one that doesn't move depending on how well others in the organization are performing. Because the goal is stable, it reduces ambiguity and gives employees a firm understanding of what they're aiming for.

Your organization's established performance goals are the ideal standard. However, employees also need to know the relevant context in which to evaluate their performance. Provide employees with performance information for their unit and the organization. If an employee is experiencing difficulties, seeing the performance of his unit and organization as a whole will give him the context necessary to make sense of his performance. If others are also struggling, this may be somewhat of a relief. If he's the only one struggling, he can focus on his self-improvement.

Putting Expectations in Writing

Put expectations in writing. Written goals, standards, and expectations reduce ambiguity for employees and give them a clear indication of what they need to achieve to advance the vision and mission of your organization and to be successful on the job. They also form the foundation for monitoring and evaluating performance.

Your Organization's Goals and Expectations

Organizations have established policies, procedures, and expectations for employees. Leveraging these is the most effective way to ensure goal alignment. First, these expectations were developed by your organization and should have been vetted through the proper channels. Many organizations and companies put their policies, procedures, and expectations through a review process that may include human resources, risk management, legal counsel, labor relations, and other relevant departments. This type of vetting process minimizes risk to you and your organization. Additionally, because these have gone through extensive organizational review and approval, you can be assured that they align with the organization's vision and strategic goals. Some of these expectations apply to all employees in the organization, and some are department- or position-specific. It's imperative that you become knowledgeable about your organization's policies, procedures, and expectations and how they impact your department and unit, as you're expected to lead your team in achieving them.

Prioritizing

Not all policies, procedures, and expectations are created equal. There are some that will rise to the top as high impact and high priority. Some you will need to refer to frequently, such as procedures and expectations for attendance, punctuality, requesting time off, completion of time cards, customer service, and the like. Others may include key performance indicators, customer service standards, organizational priorities, major initiatives, and corporate culture. Go through established policies, procedures, and expectations and prioritize them according to the frequency of use, level of impact on employee performance ratings, and the level of priority for your organization, department, and manager. Once you have gone through this process, determine which are the most important for your team. This doesn't mean you can ignore all the others; however, this prioritization process helps you focus your team's time, talent, and energy on the goals that matter the most.

The Expectations Packet

Take your organization's high-impact and high-priority policies, procedures, goals, and expectations and bundle them to create an expectations packet. Don't just hand the packet to employees and ask them to read it. If you do this, they may set it aside and not review it. Instead, take the time to discuss the expectations with your team and answer questions.

> *Documentation Tip: Document the issuance of the expectations packet by having the employee sign and date an itemized Acknowledgment of Receipt (Appendix A). File a copy of the form in the employee's file and keep copies of the expectations.*

Seeking Guidance

Obtain approval from your manager, human resources, legal counsel, or other experts as appropriate for your organization before issuing written expectations and using any documentation forms or templates. These experts can guide you on your organization's protocol and approval process for the development and issuance of documents related to human resources. They will let you know if the language you use is appropriate and will help you minimize risk.

Alex's Priorities

Vic had a solid understanding of the performance indicators that were important to Alex. She had been clear from the onset. When she started supervising Vic and the rest of the Youth Employment Program Leadership Team four months ago, she had laid out her expectations. She had even given them these expectations in writing and had emphasized the organization's priority goals:

Goal 1 – Job Placement

"Place 90% of program applicants into part-time jobs within 30 calendar days of the application date."

Goal 2 – Job Retention

"Ensure 75% of the youth placed into jobs retain their jobs for 90 calendar days or more."

Goal 3 – Customer Complaint Prevention

"Provide excellent customer service to ensure receipt of zero valid customer complaints."

Vic knew Alex was big on both performance and customer service, so he did what he could to keep her happy. And, since the monthly performance reports published by Alex's quality coordinator focused on the job placement and retention goals, that's what Vic emphasized with his team. It's what Alex would use to rate Vic's performance.

Vic's consistent focus on his team's job placement and retention goals had positive results. His team was the top performing in the program two months in a row and was in the running for a third month. Until recently, Vic's team had also been meeting the customer complaint prevention goal of having zero valid complaints each month.

Vic had always used his charming personality to appease customers and keep their complaints from elevating. But this last one had made it past him, and now Alex wanted Vic to account for all the complaints received. What a waste of time. Vic had better things to do than to babysit his staff. He was busy doing his job—making sure his team was the best at job placement and retention. He didn't have time to waste with Mary's complaints. To make matters worse, Alex was forcing him to meet with Mary and document the conversation. Like he had nothing else to do.

Why couldn't Alex just leave him alone like Tim, his previous manager, had done? Tim had never wanted to be bothered with customer complaints. As long as the numbers looked good and the CEO and board were happy, that was all Tim had cared about. Things were good then.

But Alex was now the one in charge of Vic's performance evaluation. Vic knew that if he was going to set himself up for promotion, he had to stay on her good side. He would meet with Mary about this latest complaint as Alex requested, but not today. He had too much on his plate. He would have to find some time on his calendar soon.

What Employees Expect from You

Expectations are a two-way street. Just as managers and supervisors have expectations of their employees, employees also have expectations of their supervisors, managers, and organizations. In addition to ensuring that your direct reports understand what you expect of them, you need to understand what they expect from you, individually and as a team. During initial and subsequent goal-directed conversations, clarify what employees expect and need from you. This will help you identify the support they need to achieve success.

In Review

Goals and expectations are the beginning of great performance. They let employees know what they're striving for. Yet, they alone are not enough. As a leader, you must inspire and unleash employee passion and communicate how your team's performance goals advance your organization's vision and greater good. Share the vision and associated goals continuously and through various means. When working with individual employees, focus on their self-development based on established performance standards, rather than comparing them to their peers. However, don't provide performance data in a vacuum. Employees need transparency. They need to see organizational and team performance data to make sense of their performance. Finally, expectations are a two-way street, and you need to understand what employees expect from you. This understanding will help you provide the support employees need to succeed.

Putting It into Action

1. Put together an expectations packet and issue it to your team.

2. If an employee is struggling with performance, start by clarifying and reinforcing expectations.

3. Sit down individually with each of your employees and ask them what they need and expect from you. Brace yourself, and don't get defensive. Regardless of how they respond, thank each of them for their feedback. They have given you valuable information you can reflect on to help you become a better leader.

Chapter 4
Monitoring: Focusing on What Matters

When the light shines on people's work, they will give their best performance.

Monitoring—measuring, observing, and reviewing work—is essential for promoting strong employee and organizational performance.[30] Leaders who monitor work quality and proactively interact with employees promote higher productivity levels.[31]

Employees will focus on that which you monitor. When you measure, observe, and review specific performance and customer service indicators, you're signaling to your team that they're a priority. Employees will read these signals and focus on delivering that which you monitor.

SUPPORTIVE ACCOUNTABILITY
LEADERSHIP™

Principles of Effective Monitoring

Employees are keenly aware of which of their many tasks, projects, activities, and performance goals you're monitoring and how often. They're also aware of when and what you're not monitoring. This awareness impacts where they will focus their effort. Take the time to measure, observe, and review the tasks, projects, activities, and goals that matter.

Keep It Fair and Transparent

For monitoring to be effective, use it to gauge how employees are performing in relation to established, known, and objective performance expectations, goals, metrics, and standards.[32] Keep the monitoring and evaluation process simple, objective, and consistent for all employees of the same job description and role. Base your monitoring activities on established standards, goals, and expectations that you have already communicated and for which you have equipped employees. As much as possible, let employees know in advance what you're monitoring. The goal of monitoring is to assess whether employees are meeting performance goals, not to surprise employees or to catch them doing something wrong. When you let your team know what you're monitoring, you focus their attention on the goals and priorities that matter to you and, most importantly, to your organization.

Monitor Group and Individual Performance

Monitor both at the group and individual level. Monitoring performance at the group level lets you know how your organization, department, section, and unit are performing. It also provides comparison data, demonstrating how well your team is performing compared to the rest of the organization and how well individuals are performing compared to your team as a whole. However, you don't need to broadcast individual performance data. Instead, share individual performance outcomes with each employee during private feedback conversations.

If you want to make an impact on employee performance, monitoring at the individual level is vital. As we reviewed in Chapter 3, "Expectations that Inspire," evaluating employee performance against well-planned, established performance goals and objectives creates a healthier workplace than comparing the performance of individual employees to that of their peers.[33] Yet, it's important to show transparency in organizational and team performance, so that employees can make sense of their performance based on the bigger picture. Also, transparency in organizational and team performance promotes higher levels of accountability for those in leadership positions.

Monitor Consistently

Monitor key performance indicators consistently and let employees know you're monitoring through continuous feedback. This feedback assures employees that your performance measurement and review process is fair and based on established performance standards and employee achievement of these standards, rather than on subjective measures. Consistent monitoring of performance also helps you build credibility with your team, as monitoring demonstrates that you're engaged as a leader to ensure their success. If done with an approach of supportive accountability, employees will view your monitoring activities as support rather than surveillance. Monitoring group and individual performance consistently and at regular intervals demonstrates fairness in performance evaluation and promotes strong performance.

The Youth Employment Program's Monitoring Tools

Alex sat in her office, reminiscing about her first day as the manager of YouthZone's Youth Employment Program. As a seasoned manager, she had joined the organization four months ago because she believed in the work the small nonprofit was doing to make a difference in young lives. She recalled her first few weeks getting the lay of the land. Alex had been satisfied with the organization's performance monitoring tools. The program had a robust automated work management system that captured progress on mission-critical performance goals by program, supervisor units, and individual employees. This data was useful in helping her leadership team focus on what mattered. But she wasn't quite satisfied with the program's customer service monitoring. Waiting for customer complaints was reactive. By the time a complaint came in, it was too late. Alex needed to get ahead of customer service weaknesses before they became major issues. She needed to find out what her program, supervisory units, and individual employees were doing well and what they could do better.

During her first couple of months at YouthZone, Alex had worked on a plan for strengthening customer service monitoring. She had received the support of her director and launched a new customer satisfaction program. It included a customer satisfaction survey that her quality coordinator had developed and off-the-shelf software she purchased to capture the data and produce reports.

It had already been a month since she had launched the program, and the youths were not providing much feedback. Also, her discovery that Vic had not shared the two complaints he had received from one of Mary's customers was concerning. Were these the only complaints that Vic had withheld from her? What about the other supervisors? Were they withholding similar issues? Not having her finger on the pulse of customer satisfaction made Alex uneasy. She needed to push for more customer feedback. She needed to encourage youths to submit their input so she could get an accurate read on the customer satisfaction levels for her program.

Ways to Monitor

There are many methods to measure, observe, and review work. Your organization should already have monitoring and evaluation tools in place. Find out what these are, become knowledgeable about how they work, and apply them to promote performance excellence.

Below are a few examples of ways to monitor.

Reviewing Performance Reports

Organizations typically use performance reports to monitor and manage mission-critical performance goals. Identify performance reports available at the organizational, unit, and individual levels. If your organization has a robust automated work management system, you may have access to pre-formatted performance reports. In some cases, you may even be able to pull custom reports using a variety of filters.

A drawback of a robust automated system is that it may have so many performance reports available that you don't know where to start. Many of these reports may be useful to someone else in your organization, but they may also distract you from focusing on key performance goals. To avoid stretching yourself and your team too thin, find out which performance goals and reports matter most to your role and will be used to rate your performance. These are the mission-critical performance goals you must focus on and reinforce continuously with your team. Learn what these reports and performance goals mean, the level of performance your team is expected to achieve, and how the data is gathered and reported to determine your team's achievement.

Master the use of relevant reports. Find out which fields in the system your team needs to complete and how this data entry impacts performance outcomes. Understanding how the system collects data and how end user actions affect performance reports will help you identify best practices. It will also equip you to teach employees how to properly use the automated system, which will impact their individual and collective performance outcomes.

Performance reports are only worthwhile if they're used to inspire great performance. Continuously focus your team on the performance outcomes revealed by these reports and how these outcomes advance your organization's vision and mission. Regularly review these reports, share organizational and unit data with your team, and discuss individual performance with each employee during your private conferences. Reports that merely gather dust won't inspire great performance.

If you don't have automated reports available to you, find out if there's an established manual mechanism to gather performance data, such as a spreadsheet or database. If not, you may need to develop one. This method of monitoring is time-consuming and inefficient. However, not having any monitoring mechanism at all is detrimental to effective performance management.

Vic Monitors His Team's Performance

Vic was passionate about his team's performance. Nothing made him happier than to see his team outshining the others in job placement and retention. The outcomes for these two performance goals were published in the Monthly Program Performance Report and the Monthly Unit Performance Report. Vic eagerly anticipated the results each month.

The goals were clear:

Goal 1 – Job Placement

"Place 90% of program applicants into part-time jobs within 30 calendar days of the application date."

Goal 2 – Job Retention

"Ensure 75% of the youth placed into jobs retain their jobs for 90 calendar days or more."

YouthZone collected and reported job placement and retention data via YouthTrak, its longstanding automated work management system. Youth employment specialists managed their work by entering progress data into YouthTrak. The system automatically calculated job placement and retention statistics by program, unit, and employee based on data entered by staff. On a daily basis, Vic queried the system and pulled up real-time performance reports for the program and his team. This helped him stay ahead of any issues affecting his numbers. His diligence in monitoring his team's performance paid off.

Today was the first working day of the month, and Vic was excited to see the final data for the previous month. He pulled up the monthly performance reports from YouthTrak. His numbers were excellent. Collectively his team of seven youth employment specialists achieved 92% job placement and 81% job retention, meeting and exceeding the goals of 90% and 75% respectively. Vic was satisfied. He had once again beaten all his peers. This was the third month in a row. Alex would surely be impressed.

> *Documentation Tip:* See Appendix B - *Monthly Program Performance Report* and Appendix C - *Monthly Unit Performance Report*. Retain copies of performance reports. You can maintain them either in the employee's file or in a centralized location, whichever is more convenient.

The Story Behind the Numbers

Performance reports don't stand alone. You need to know the story behind the numbers. While performance reports give you quantitative information about how your team and individual employees are performing, there's also a qualitative side to data. This qualitative side can't be measured or quantified, but rather provides information about performance qualities, constraints, and other relevant information. Together, quantitative and qualitative data paint a complete picture of organizational, team, and individual performance. You can't just rely on quantitative data to assess performance. For an accurate and fair assessment, you need to take into account the story behind the numbers.

The Low Producer

The manager of a fast-paced office was reviewing the weekly productivity reports for a team of three payment processing clerks who were under his indirect supervision. The reports showed that two of the clerks processed an acceptable number of payments for the week. However, the third clerk had only achieved half the productivity level in comparison to her peers. The manager also reviewed a report from the company's employee timekeeping system. It showed that all three clerks had worked a 40-hour workweek. As far as the manager was concerned, the third clerk was drastically underperforming.

Upset, he called the payment center supervisor to his office and ranted about how the supervisor wasn't doing her job. He complained that she had let the employee underperform for an entire week without bringing it to his attention. She had wasted company time and money and had failed to hold the employee accountable.

The supervisor listened intently until the manager was done. Then, in a professional manner, she explained that the clerk with the lowest productivity numbers was actually her highest producer. Under normal circumstances, this clerk consistently processed about 25% more payments than the other two clerks did.

The reason the clerk's work seemed low that particular week was that she was working on the special project the manager had requested. The last two weeks had been slower than usual at the payment center, so the supervisor had assigned the clerk the project to help in her development. The great news was that clerk had completed the project a week ahead of the deadline and had returned to the payment center. The supervisor was reviewing the final product, and it would be on the manager's desk by close of business.

The manager felt embarrassed. He had jumped to conclusions based solely on the data without first trying to get the story behind the numbers. Even worse, in his frustration, his approach had been one of unsupportive accountability.

Observations

As a monitoring tool, observations are one way to get the story behind the numbers. They can help you identify factors contributing to high and low performance. When you compare observations to performance reports, you can determine which employees are more efficient and which may be struggling. You can use this information to provide training and support to those who need it. Observations can also help you identify process deficiencies, such as bottlenecks, unnecessary hand-offs, duplication of effort, and other issues that may affect performance. Furthermore, observations can help you determine the need for tools, equipment, and other resources.

Check your data and assumptions against observations and other relevant information. Talk to key people at various stages of the process. Performance issues are not always about frontline employees. Sometimes they're about systems, processes, leadership, support needs, or a combination of these.

Transparency is Vital. Observations can feel intrusive to your employees, especially if you're new to the team. To mitigate these concerns, let employees know in advance that you will be observing, and let them know the reason. Employees will appreciate your transparency. Often, they will appreciate that you have taken an interest in what they do and that you intend to help them. If you approach the observation process with a mindset of support, it can also be a step in building employee trust.

Observation May Alter Employee Behavior. Employees may change their behavior and performance during your observations. They may speed up their work or become more diligent in their quality than is customary for them. However, this is of no concern. The reason you're observing is to get the story behind the numbers. This includes identifying opportunities for improvement, providing support, and implementing solutions. Even if employees change their behavior during your observations, you should still be able to gain some helpful insights. Getting a closer view of how the work gets done will provide you the additional context from which to support, monitor, and evaluate employee performance. You can also glean best practices from top performers and use these to assist those who are struggling in the same role.

The Speed of Light

As a seasoned manager, I transferred to a large office where employees were facing environmental challenges to performance. Prior to this, I worked for several years in various operations management roles with multiple high-volume offices serving the same customer base. The offices had different nuances, team dynamics, and environmental influences. Getting to know each of these operations was vital to providing employees with supportive accountability.

Now in a new office, I wanted to get a firsthand feel for the challenges employees were facing. Therefore, I asked the leadership team to arrange for me to informally job shadow three employees—a high performer, an employee meeting expectations, and an employee who was struggling. When scheduling me to job shadow the employee who was struggling, the leadership team informed me that the employee had quality issues and was slow at processing work. However, when I shadowed the supposedly low-performing employee, I was surprised to see the work processed with attention to detail and notable speed. I shared my observations with the supervisors of the team, who were convinced I had observed another worker by mistake. They investigated, and there was no mistake. When the light shines on people's work, they will give their best performance.

Job Shadowing Employees

Job shadowing employees is one form of observation. You can use it as part of your development plan when you start in a new position or role. You can also use it to help with employee performance improvement.

Job Shadowing for Your Self-Development. As soon as you report to a new leadership assignment, quickly learn the inner workings of your operations. Don't wait for your manager to prepare a learning plan for you. Demonstrate ownership, initiative, and a sense of urgency by scheduling employee job shadowing as part of your training plan and letting your direct manager know. Job shadowing employees as they work is an excellent way for you to learn about the people, products, processes, and services under your oversight. If you're new to the role, job shadowing employees will help you learn your process flow and how the work gets done. If you're a seasoned leader experienced in the same role but transitioning to another unit, section, office, or division, job shadowing your new team will help you understand the nuances of your new environment. In either case, job shadowing will help you understand what your frontline employees actually do. It will give you a profound appreciation for the successes and challenges employees experience every day. Equipped with this knowledge, you will be in a much better position to provide supportive accountability.

Job Shadowing for Performance Improvement. Job shadowing employees is also a good tool to help employees improve their performance. If you have employees with significant challenges in their work that they haven't been able to correct in spite of coaching, training, and other support, it may be time to conduct employee job shadowing.

People are individuals, and what works for one person may not work for another. Job shadowing employees who are struggling can help you gain insight into their specific strengths, weaknesses, challenges, and support needs.

Here are four steps you can take to help employees improve performance through employee job shadowing:

1. **Notify the Employee in Advance** – Let the employee know that you would like to help him improve his performance through job shadowing and explain what it will involve. Emphasize that you intend to use this as a support

to the employee and your goal is the employee's success. Ask the employee if he has any questions and provide candid but caring answers.

2. **Observe** – During your job shadowing, observe and ask questions, but don't give feedback. This isn't a coaching moment. It's an observation moment. Take notes on what the employee is doing well and what he can improve. Give some thought to what you will observe. Will you be looking at the employee's organizational skills? Are you evaluating the employee's ability to schedule activities and follow through? What are the best practices for your industry? At the minimum, make a list of what is essential in the employee's line of work, but allow for some flexibility. You never know what you may encounter, as each person is unique.

3. **Reflect and Report** – After employee job shadowing is complete, reflect on your discoveries and write your observations down in a simple report. What did the employee do well? What could the employee do differently? Are there any tips, tools, or training you can provide the employee to make his work easier? Use neutral and uplifting language in the report and emphasize the positive. The goal of employee job shadowing is to help the employee improve, not to damage his self-esteem. The report should have all the appropriate information: date of job shadowing, employee name, observations, recommendations, and your signature and date.

4. **Provide Performance Feedback** – Engage the employee in a performance conversation. You can read more about this in Chapter 6, "Best Practices in Performance Feedback," and Chapter 7, "Leading Performance Improvement Conversations." Document the conversation.

> *Documentation Tip: See Appendix K - Conversation Notes Template. File a copy of your conversation notes in the employee's file.*

Structured Observations to Monitor Performance

You can also use formal observations to monitor performance and customer interactions. The key is to use a structured observation tool that focuses on predetermined, objective criteria and employs a rating rubric to evaluate performance and provide feedback. You can use observations for various types of work. You can observe training, customer interactions, data entry, driving, task processing, and more. Conducting formal, structured observations of employees at work is essential for employees whose work involves interactions with others, such as receptionists, social workers, counter attendants, trainers, bank tellers, and telephone service agents. In Chapter 5, "Measuring Customer Service," I provide more information on how to use observations to help improve customer service.

Walking the Floor

Observations can also be informal and as simple as walking around, watching, listening, and asking questions. Walk around various work areas and observe employees. Observe their work, their conversations, their focus, their interactions, their frustrations, and their successes. Through these informal observations, you will get a feel for the atmosphere in your office. If a team member wants to ask you a question while you're walking around, take the time to listen and respond. These conversations will put you in touch with the reality your workforce is experiencing, help you get to know employees, and provide a glimpse into the support needs of your team. However, the information you gain from walking the floor is only helpful if you act on it. Failure to acknowledge and follow through on employees' support needs and requests will diminish their trust for you, impact your credibility, and discourage employees from further reaching out to you for assistance.

Talking with Employees

Another way for you to informally assess how employees are doing is to talk with them frequently. Ask them how things are going. What is going well in their jobs? What are they happy about? What isn't going so well? What are their challenges? What help do they need? You can glean plenty of information from simple conversations, a few questions, and a lot of listening. Talking with employees helps you learn more about their needs, priorities, hopes, dreams, fears, and concerns. The more you learn about people, the more you can support them, demonstrate you care, and build trust.

In Review

Monitoring is a powerful tool to focus employees on what matters most. To get the most out of your monitoring activities, keep them fair, objective, and transparent for all employees; monitor both at the individual and group level; and monitor consistently. Employees know what you're monitoring and how frequently. Thus, employees will focus their energy and efforts on the goals, objectives, and tasks you're reviewing. Use this performance management element to give them clarity, reinforce expectations, and identify the support you can provide. These essential monitoring principles will help you promote successful performance outcomes for the individual, the team, and the organization.

Putting It into Action

1. Make a list of the critical performance indicators for your team and identify the mission-critical reports available to track individual and team performance for each of these indicators.

2. Walk the floor on a regular basis to observe performance and talk to team members.

3. If you have an employee who is struggling, review the appropriate performance reports and evaluate the need for observations.

Chapter 5
Measuring Customer Service

"If you really want good customer service, you have to treat your employees as your number one customer and value and respect them and do everything you can to help them be successful."

– Wendi Pomerance Brick, President & CEO of
Customer Service Advantage, Inc.

C ustomer service excellence is like any other mission-critical performance goal. Monitor it at the organizational, team, and individual levels. To achieve customer service excellence, continuously assess the way your team delivers the goods.

DOCUMENTATION   EXPECTATIONS

ACCOUNTABILITY   SUPPORTIVE   MONITORING
ACCOUNTABILITY

RECOGNITION   FEEDBACK

SUPPORT

SUPPORTIVE ACCOUNTABILITY
LEADERSHIP™

Getting Customer Feedback

The number one determinant of customer service excellence is the customer experience. Customers are in a unique position to tell you if their experience was indeed excellent or if it was lacking. To assess how well your organization is doing in the area of customer service, ask your customers. The customer satisfaction survey is one way you can ask them for their feedback.

Customer Satisfaction Surveys

You can use customer satisfaction surveys to ask customers what they think. Like all performance monitoring tools, surveys are also a way to measure whether or not you, employees, and your organization are meeting established performance expectations. Therefore, your survey questions must be tailored to measure customer and organizational expectations and to align with your industry's standards.

As you develop your surveys, write your questions so you can use them later to produce customer service reports. Think about the type of data that's necessary for you to improve your people, products, processes, and service, and how this data can be displayed on reports and used effectively. Keep in mind that you will need these reports to identify trends over time, improve products and service, and provide meaningful feedback to employees. Once you have the framework for your reports, develop the questions that will populate these reports.

Survey Answer Formats

There are two common survey answer formats, the "Likert scale" and the "control list format."

The Likert Scale. Hieberger and Robbins explained that rating scales are frequently used in customer satisfaction surveys and that the most common is the Likert scale. The Likert scale captures degrees of satisfaction. For instance, you can use a 5-point Likert scale, or a scale from 1 to 5, enabling respondents to rate their experience based on five levels of satisfaction. Customers could select from one of the following responses:

1 – Strongly Disagree

2 – Disagree

3 – No Opinion

4 – Agree

5 – Strongly Agree[34]

Since this 5-point Likert scale uses an odd number of responses, it allows customers to select a neutral answer.

However, Hieberger and Robbins wrote that you can also use Likert scales with an "even number of levels (choices), forcing the respondent to make a directional (non-neutral) choice."[35] For instance, the following 4-point Likert scale would require customers to indicate whether or not they were satisfied:

1 – Strongly Disagree

2 – Disagree

3 – Agree

4 – Strongly Agree

The Control List Format. Lucian et al. explain the control list format, where customers would have to choose between "yes" and "no." While this "yes" and "no" format is much simpler, it's not as reliable as the 5-point Likert scale. Lucian et al. wrote, "Statistically, the two answer options scales have a smaller reliability than scales with five answer options (Lissitz and Green, 1975)."[36]

If possible, use a 5-point Likert scale.

Comments Section. Include a free-form comments section where customers can either expand on the reasoning behind their ratings or share something that doesn't fit into your survey questions.

Make this section voluntary. If you make it mandatory and customers don't want to complete it, they will most likely abandon the survey.

Open-Ended Questions. You can also use open-ended questions, where you allow customers to enter free-form responses instead of having to select from predetermined choices. Although open-ended questions require more work to quantify, they let customers express their opinions freely. Open-ended questions are invaluable and can provide a wealth of information that will help you improve your people, products, processes, and service and provide meaningful feedback to employees. Evaluate if open-ended questions are feasible and suitable for your situation.

Tips for Drafting Survey Questions

Lucian et al. provide the following tips for drafting survey questions to prevent customer confusion:

Brief. Keep the survey questions short. Lengthy questions affect readability and comprehension.

Clear. Be specific in your questions. Don't use ambiguous language. Customers need to know precisely what the survey is asking so they can answer appropriately.

Single Factor. Only ask about one dimension of service at a time. Avoid asking about multiple factors in one question, as this could cause customer frustration and hinder analysis. The customer may want to respond differently to each element, but the question format wouldn't allow them to do so.[37] If respondents provide suggestions for improvement in a multiple-factor question, you may have difficulty determining which factor to address.

Customers Don't Always Respond to Surveys

Regardless of how well-developed the survey format may be, many customers won't respond. Return rates for external customer satisfaction surveys are usually low. Customer satisfaction experts report conflicting information regarding response rates, ranging from 10% to 40%. However, 40% is optimistic. Typically, the return rate is on the lower side of the range.

In any case, many customers won't provide feedback unless their experience is either so positive or so negative that they're compelled to tell their story. An experience that merely meets expectations usually isn't enough for customers to take the time to provide feedback. Also, some dissatisfied customers won't provide negative feedback. Instead, they will send your organization a strong message by not returning. For private companies, this can translate to lost revenue and bad public relations. For government and government-contracted organizations whose customers have no other options for services, dissatisfied customers may find other avenues to express their frustrations. These may include contacting the top executives, advocacy organizations, or their elected officials, or posting on social media. This can throw government agencies into a reactive mode as they put out the fires that ensue. For all types of organizations, poor customer service is a bad way of doing business.

Be proactive in your customer service efforts. Focus on increasing the amount of customer feedback you receive. The more input you collect, the more you will understand your customers' experience. You will have enough information to adequately determine patterns and trends by office, organizational unit, and individual. This information will help you develop targeted solutions to deliver world-class customer service. The easier you make it for customers to give feedback, the more likely you will receive it.

The SAM Method for Getting More Customer Feedback

You can use the **SAM method** to make it easy for customers to provide feedback. SAM stands for:

S – Simple
A – Accessible
M – Multiple Formats and Pathways

S - Simple

Keep your feedback process simple. Don't make your surveys too long, too complicated, or too cumbersome to complete, or customers will stop midstream and abandon the survey. Don't make your questionnaires difficult to understand, or they will either miss the point of your questions in their responses or not answer at all.

A - Accessible

Make your feedback methods and pathways accessible. Don't make your customers click through multiple pages on your website to find out how to provide feedback. Instead, post feedback opportunities prominently. Display the information everywhere you can. Feedback methods and pathways are useless if customers can't locate them.

M - Multiple Formats and Pathways

People are individuals. One size doesn't fit all. Some customers prefer online submission. Others like to submit their feedback via telephone or on paper. Provide a variety of formats and pathways for customers to express their opinions about your people, products, processes, and service.

Dedicated Chat, Email, and Phone Number

One of the easiest ways to secure customer feedback is to have a dedicated chat line, email address, and phone number where customers can express their feelings and opinions. Having these dedicated pathways allows customers to provide feedback on their own terms without the limitations of pre-formatted questions. Some customers don't want to be bothered with questionnaires and prefer an avenue for free expression. You need to provide it. This type of forum is especially important when a customer is unhappy, frustrated, or irate. When emotions run high, customers don't want to go through a series of questions before they can vent about their experience.

Dedicated email addresses and phone numbers are perfect vehicles for free expression. They're accessible to customers 24 hours a day, 7 days a week. It's best to have a live body that instantly responds to emails and answers telephone calls. However, you may not have the budget to answer emails instantly or cover the phones 24/7. At a minimum, be prepared to accept customer messages and be responsive to feedback. Set up automatic email replies and phone greetings that immediately acknowledge receipt of the message. If the customer is dissatisfied with your product or service, add the human touch by returning the contact within one business day to resolve the issue. Responding to customer complaints promptly is vital for maintaining credibility and customer trust.

Customers will express their concerns regardless of whether or not you offer them the opportunity to do so. You can either provide them a forum to vent directly to you or wait for them to blast your organization through social media, consumer watchdog agencies, friends, family, or their elected officials. In any case, your organization's reputation is at stake.

Alex Increases Customer Feedback

It was one month after the launch of the new customer satisfaction program. Sam, the Youth Employment Program's quality coordinator, walked into her office with a report in his hand.

"Here it is, Alex. Our first official Monthly Customer Satisfaction Report," Sam said as he handed Alex the report. "Sorry it took me so long to get it to you, but I wanted to double-check the data. The numbers looked low. I didn't think we'd captured all the surveys. But I double-checked, and you were right. We're not getting much feedback."

"Okay then," Alex said, "let's talk about how we can increase the amount of customer feedback we're getting."

Sam recommended some adjustments to the customer satisfaction program to make it simple, accessible, and available through multiple formats and pathways. Alex liked and adopted many of the suggestions.

In the revised program, the youths could submit free-form comments by email, telephone, or in person. Alex didn't have the budget to hire additional employees to provide chat options. However, in addition to free-form feedback, youths could submit customer satisfaction surveys online, in person, through U.S. mail, via email, or by telephone.

To raise awareness among program youth, Sam advertised these feedback methods and pathways. He posted the information on each page of the Youth Employment Program's website and in customer correspondence, brochures, flyers, posters, and other documents. He added a link to this information below the email signature lines of all Youth Employment Program employees. Sam also encouraged program staff to verbally share information about how to submit feedback at the various stages of the youths' participation in the program. He displayed informational posters in the high-traffic areas of the three program sites. He placed paper copies at key customer contact points, including reception areas, interview stations, classrooms, service counters, and information booths.

Collecting Customer Satisfaction Data

With Alex's approval, Sam also strengthened the process for collecting customer satisfaction information using the off-the-shelf software Alex had purchased when she first implemented the program. With the revised process, youths could complete their surveys online using survey software or over the telephone using touch-tone technology. Alex also installed customer service kiosks in all her program lobbies so the youths could complete an electronic survey on-site.

If they elected to submit paper surveys rather than using the available technology, designated clerks manually entered the data and comments into the survey software. Youths could email scanned copies of the paper surveys. They also had the option of dropping off the manual surveys at one of the locked drop boxes in customer lobbies or handing them to one of the employees.

The survey software Alex purchased allowed Alex, Sam, and supervisors to pull real-time reports and refine their search results by program, unit, and individual employee. Access to copies of the surveys and individual-level reports was restricted to managers, supervisors, and designated support staff via user IDs and passwords. These system security protocols safeguarded the confidentiality of employee-specific data and customer complaints.

The Customer Satisfaction Survey

When Alex had initially launched the customer satisfaction program, Sam had developed a survey that focused on four areas of service—professionalism, promptness, responsiveness, and assistance. Since the questionnaire was fairly simple, Alex and Sam agreed to continue using it without any revisions. Alex knew that no one in the organization had expertise in survey development. Also, her budget didn't allow her to outsource this task. Therefore, she and Sam had evaluated sample surveys from other organizations during the planning phase.

The Complaint Process

Before Alex implemented the adjustments to the customer satisfaction program, the Youth Employment Program had a lax complaint process. Customers would complain to someone in the program, and the information was given to the appropriate supervisor. Alex didn't get involved unless the complaint was escalated. She changed this.

The revisions Alex and Sam implemented promoted transparency. Now, when customer complaints were received, either through a survey or a free-form submission, a designated clerk would enter the feedback into the organization's customer survey software. The software would automatically alert the employee's supervisor. Sam would retrieve the data and provide monthly customer satisfaction reports to Alex, Sam, and the entire leadership team by program, unit, and individual employee. The software also allowed Alex and the team to pull real-time reports as often as necessary.

Supervisor and Employee Expectations

Depending on the nature of the complaint, Alex expected her supervisors to contact the customer within one business day to start working on the resolution unless the customer preferred no contact. In either case, Alex made sure her supervisors knew the issue needed to be addressed with the individual employee to reinforce customer service expectations and teach customer service excellence. She developed written customer service expectations to ensure supervisors and employees understood their roles and responsibilities.

As part of these written expectations, Alex introduced a second customer service goal. She kept the original goal of receiving zero valid customer complaints each month, but she added the following:

Goal 4 – Customer Satisfaction

"On a monthly and yearly basis, achieve an average customer satisfaction rating of 4 or higher in all customer satisfaction areas measured."

This last goal provided a proactive approach to customer service feedback. The Youth Employment Program was now actively seeking input from its customers, the youth that depended on their services. With these efforts to simplify the feedback process and to raise youth awareness about it, the feedback started coming in.

Documentation Tip: See Appendix E – Customer Satisfaction Survey. File copies of customer surveys in the employee's file.

Mystery Shopping Programs

Mystery shopping is another effective method for measuring customer satisfaction.

Wendi Pomerance Brick has extensive experience designing and conducting mystery shopping programs. Wendi is the President and CEO of Customer Service Advantage, Inc. and the author of *The Science of Service: Six Essential Elements for Creating a Culture of Service in the Public Sector.* As a customer service expert with over 25 years' experience in the field, I interviewed Wendi regarding her perspective about using mystery shopping as a customer service monitoring tool.[38]

What Is Mystery Shopping?

Wendi emphasized, "Mystery shopping is a tool to help organizations meet the performance metrics that they have already established." She explained that there are two basic types of mystery shopping programs. One involves evaluating the process. The mystery shopper pretends to be an actual customer, goes through the entire process, and evaluates the experience. Wendi emphasized that this type of mystery shopping is difficult to accomplish, takes a significant amount of time and resources, and generally will result in such a small sample size it doesn't yield sufficient results to justify a good return on investment. For these reasons, she doesn't recommend shopping the process in most cases or relying on this approach as the only measurement for gathering performance data.[39]

Therefore, our interview focused on the second type of mystery shopping, which involves shopping three different types of initial contacts: emails, phone calls, and in person. In this type of mystery shopping, the mystery shopper also pretends to be a customer but only evaluates the initial contact with an employee. Organizations can measure the "first impressions" and gather much larger data pools from which to develop continuous improvement programs.[40]

Four Essential Elements of Mystery Shopping

Wendi explained that there are four vital elements required for the successful mystery shopping of contacts.

Element 1 – It Shouldn't Be a Mystery. The most essential element of a mystery shopping program is that "it shouldn't be a mystery." Wendi stressed, "Everyone should know this is coming. I tell everyone. I write emails. I say it at staff meetings. 'We're going to be mystery shopped. This is how you get fives (on the evaluations). This is what we're looking for.' I want everyone to get fives. I'm not looking for people to fail. I'm trying to emphasize certain behaviors in the workplace. It's a training tool… The fact that you're doing the program should never be a surprise, because then it's very *big brotherish*, like you're looking over people's shoulders. Being mystery shopped is very uncomfortable. Staff can think you're assuming they're doing something wrong. That would create a negative culture, not a culture of learning and service. If you really want good customer service, you have to treat your employees as your number one customer and value and respect them and do everything you can to help them be successful. You never ever want to set up a negative work environment."[41]

Element 2 – Follow-Up. Wendi said, "Part of making a shopping program successful is follow-up. In any performance measurement program—any measuring, monitoring, any survey, anything—there's literally no point in doing it, if you don't follow up. You're doing it for a reason: to learn something. You must implement changes after you do the program, especially if you're going to do it again. Let's say I do mystery shopping once a year. Before I do it again, I better implement changes and help people get fives, if they didn't already. Otherwise, what was the point?"[42]

Element 3 – Trending Over Time. Wendi shared, "Another valuable gain from measurement programs is the trend over time. You want to do it three, four, or five times to see if you're trending in the right direction. Not just once. Once is just a baseline."[43]

Element 4 – Neutrality and Objectivity. Wendi highlighted, "You also want to make sure that whoever is doing the shopping is a neutral, objective person." She explained that conducting a neutral internal mystery shopping program is more feasible for larger organizations. Providing an example of a program she implemented for a larger organization, she said, "There were 10,000 employees. And you had a (centralized group) that was not part of any of the other groups and was completely objective. They had the assignment of (mystery shopping) objectively. During their mystery shopper training, this objectiveness must be emphasized." For companies and organizations that are unable to find a neutral third party to conduct the mystery shopping, she suggested hiring an external firm. [44]

Outsourcing Mystery Shopping

Wendi emphasized that whether or not to outsource mystery shopping is situational. She said, "It really depends on the organization, the size, the flavor, the culture, if they have neutrality, or if they don't."[45]

Wendi noted that if an organization doesn't have a budget to outsource mystery shopping, it could develop and implement its own program. However, she cautioned that budget shouldn't be the only consideration, as it takes time, a significant amount of planning, an understanding of surveying technique, execution, and resources to have an effective program. She said, "It's a labor-intensive program if you're going to do it internally. So if you are asking staff to do this as a collateral duty, and taking time away from their core functions, are you really saving money, and will it cause delays, etc. in other areas?" She suggested that if organizations are short-staffed or don't have the expertise, it may be worthwhile to invest in outsourcing.[46]

For more information about Wendi and Customer Service Advantage, Inc., please visit www.thecsaedge.com.

Analyzing the Data

As you make customer feedback mechanisms simple and accessible using multiple formats and pathways, your customers will start responding. You will need a structured system in place to analyze the data you receive.

Survey Software

For automated surveys, you can use software that allows you to customize your questions, gather customer responses, and create reports. Many off-the-shelf products on the market have built-in reports you can quickly deploy. Conduct an internet search using the keywords "survey software," and you will discover an array of options available at various price points. Free software is available for a limited number of surveys, a limited number of respondents, or both. Other software provides more bells and whistles and more capacity, but at a higher cost.

Data Collection Mechanism

Have your data collection and reporting process in place before you launch your surveys. Who will gather the questionnaires and how? What tool will you use to collect and report the data? Will you use survey software, a database, or a spreadsheet? Who will perform the data entry?

Designing Reports

Before you develop your surveys and data collection mechanism, map out the reports you need to ensure you're collecting the required data elements. Ideally, your reports should slice the data at several levels, such as departments, locations, units, and individuals. This allows you to pinpoint where support and accountability are most needed.

Incorporate quantitative data through numeric ratings and qualitative information through customer comments. If you make direct contact with the customer and gather any additional insights, integrate these into your tracking mechanism. Written comments will be instrumental in making sense of the data.

Also, think about how to display the data. Looking at nothing but numbers is boring and takes longer to analyze and interpret.

Using colorful pie charts and graphs is visually appealing, conveys the message much faster, and makes the information more memorable and impactful. Strong visuals help you analyze the data quickly to determine how well your organization is performing. Similarly, they make the data more tangible and usable during feedback conversations.

Vic's Individual Conference with Alex

It was the first week of June, and Vic was eager to meet with Alex for their monthly conference. He was ready to impress her with his team's excellent May performance. For the third month in a row, he had beaten every single unit in the program on job placement and retention.

Vic walked into Alex's office with his performance reports in hand. She was already waiting for him, sitting at the small table in front of her desk, a folder and notebook lying in front of her and a pen in hand.

"Good morning, Vic." Alex greeted him and asked him to have a seat.

Vic sat down and went over his team's performance reports with Alex, as she listened and took notes.

"That's very impressive, Vic," Alex affirmed. "I appreciate your consistency in focusing your team on both job placement and job retention. It makes a big difference for the youths and, in many cases, for their families too. And everything we do is about their success, which brings me to customer service."

Alex opened her folder and pulled out a small packet of stapled papers. "Have you had a chance to take a look at our new customer satisfaction reports?" Alex handed Vic copies of the reports.

"Uh…no. Not yet," Vic answered. "I've been super busy pulling performance data for my team."

Alex continued. "Sam pulled them for me this morning. He'll be emailing them to the entire leadership team once a month. However, the data is available for you to access on demand. Go ahead and take a few minutes to review the reports. I'd like us to discuss them."

Vic looked over the reports. He paid particular attention to his Unit Customer Satisfaction Report. Overall, the numbers looked good.

Alex asked Vic, "What do you think about your unit's report?"

Vic looked at it more closely. "Overall, my team is doing good work in customer service. We met the goals in all areas measured and did particularly well in promptness and assistance."

"Yes, I agree," said Alex. "Your team is doing very well overall. But what do you think about each team member's performance?"

"Well," said Vic. "Most are in good shape. Most are doing well, but it looks like Mary's not meeting in responsiveness and is struggling quite a bit in professionalism."

"And what do you think about that?" Alex asked.

"She needs to improve, of course," Vic replied.

"And what can you do to help her improve?" Alex's questions continued coming.

"Maybe she can take some kind of training," Vic suggested. "Is that possible?"

"Yes, it's possible," Alex affirmed. "But there's much more to helping her improve her customer service than sending her to training. This isn't the first time that she's had issues with customer service. Remember the girl who wrote the letter complaining about Mary last month? And the same girl had already complained to you twice about Mary's rudeness before sending the letter."

"Yes, I remember," acknowledged Vic.

Alex clarified. "This is now a pattern. And I'm concerned that Mary received negative customer satisfaction surveys in spite of the conversation you had with her last month about the letter."

"About that," Vic interjected.

"Yes?" Alex asked.

"I didn't actually get the chance to talk to her about the letter," Vic said.

"What?" Alex asked in disbelief.

"Yeah...I, uh...was going to...but—"

"Vic, this isn't good," Alex interrupted. "By not giving Mary immediate feedback about the complaint letter, as you and I had agreed you would, you didn't give her an opportunity to correct her customer service. Now she's received more complaints. It's really unfair to her."

Vic felt the temperature rising in Alex's office. He grabbed his collar, trying to cool off, but to no avail.

"I'm sorry, Alex. I just got so busy."

"Vic, I know you're busy. And you work hard to ensure your team is on top of their game when it comes to job placement and job retention. But customer service is important too. What makes this even more concerning is that the new customer service software generated alerts for you as soon as the complaints were logged in. Why didn't you act on them?"

Vic answered, "I didn't know what to do with them."

"You could have asked me, and I could have guided you," Alex emphasized. "When you and I talked about Mary's complaint letter, I clearly explained that you were expected to inform me when you receive complaints, and that didn't happen."

Vic and Alex were both quiet for a moment. Alex's face was serious by now. Her voice was lower and slower than usual. She had full composure, but Vic knew she was unhappy.

Alex broke the silence. "An important part of your job is to ensure that your staff is meeting all performance indicators, including those related to customer service. As her supervisor, you need to be honest with Mary and let her know she needs to improve. Now, not only will you need to talk to Mary about her low ratings in her Customer Satisfaction Report, but you'll also need to provide her feedback about the complaint letter I received a whole month ago."

By now Vic was rubbing the back of his neck. Seeing that Vic was uncomfortable, Alex softened her approach and coached him on next steps. Mary's Employee Customer Satisfaction Report had low scores in professionalism and responsiveness. However, the surveys didn't provide sufficient information for Vic to offer Mary specific feedback.

So Alex asked Vic to conduct observations of Mary's customer interactions. Alex gave Vic copies of the Customer Interaction Observation Tool and the Observation Summary Report that Sam had developed. He agreed to observe three interviews and document the results using the tools.

Alex set up a follow-up meeting with Vic to review his observations and discuss the approach he would take in providing Mary feedback. This time Alex would work with Vic from start to finish until he had documented the entire process. She would make sure he followed through.

Vic sped out of Alex's office. That hadn't gone well at all. Alex was definitely unhappy about this whole customer service thing. Now she was on him, and Vic had to waste more time observing Mary's interactions and talking to her about complaints. This whole mess could jeopardize his promotion. Ugh! Everything had been fine before Alex got here.

Documentation Tip: See Appendix F – Unit Customer Satisfaction Report; Appendix G – Employee Customer Satisfaction Report; Appendix H – Customer Interaction Observation Tool; and Appendix I – Observations Summary Report. Maintain copies of performance reports, observation tools, and summaries.

Customer Satisfaction Surveys Don't Always Provide Details

Customer satisfaction surveys are an effective method for evaluating individual employee performance. However, they alone are not always sufficient for you to make a complete and accurate assessment. Customers don't always provide their input, even when asked. Sometimes you won't receive feedback regarding all the members of your team. When customers do provide feedback for specific employees, it may or may not contain sufficient detail to assess their performance and coach them, if necessary. Due to these limitations, customer satisfaction surveys shouldn't be your only method for monitoring and evaluating customer service.

Vic Observes Mary's Interactions

Vic observed three of Mary's interviews, recorded his findings on the Customer Interaction Observation Tool, and summarized the results of on the Observation Summary Report. He discovered that Mary was efficient at gathering information during her interactions; she completed her interviews quickly and processed a high volume of work. But because she rushed her customers, her interpersonal approach suffered.

Documentation Tip: Using standardized tools to conduct observations and provide feedback helps you remain consistent, objective, and fair. File copies of your completed observation tools and summaries in the employee's file.

Following Up with Your Customers

If you ask your customers for feedback and they take the time to provide it, follow up with them. Add a question to the customer satisfaction survey asking if they wish to be contacted. Giving customers a choice respects their time, honors their wishes, and lets them know their feedback is valued. If they request a response, follow through. Manage customer expectations by specifying your turnaround time for addressing inquiries and concerns. Whatever you promise, make sure you deliver. However, don't take more than one business day to respond. You can't expect customers to be patient, especially if they need a problem resolved.

Sharing Customer Service Feedback

Customer feedback is a valuable instrument for employee performance management. It's also a great tool for staff development. The information provided by customers is vital to help you achieve customer service excellence. Share it with employees promptly, honestly, and in the spirit of supportive accountability.

In Review

Customer service, like any other chief performance indicator, must be measured and assessed on a regular basis. There are many ways to monitor customer service. The most important is to ask customers directly about their experience in receiving goods and services from your organization. The problem is that it's not easy to obtain this input, as customers don't tend to give feedback unless their experience was noteworthy, whether negative or positive. Without sufficient customer feedback, you're not able to adequately assess customer satisfaction levels at the organizational, team, and individual levels. To encourage more feedback, use the SAM method, keeping customer feedback simple and accessible, and using multiple formats and pathways. Also, conduct direct observations of employees' in-person and telephone interactions with customers or implement a mystery shopper–type program. The best approach is to use a variety of monitoring methods to assess your customer service. This will yield a broader and deeper blend of information that can help you focus your resources where they're needed the most.

Putting It into Action

1. Develop a simple customer satisfaction survey using a 5-point Likert scale answer format. Make the survey brief and clear, and use single-factor questions.

2. Develop a customer interaction observation tool.

3. If you have an employee who is struggling with customer service:

   ◦ Analyze positive and negative customer feedback trends for the employee,

   ◦ Determine if you need to conduct customer interaction observations and consult with your manager or human resources expert,

   ◦ Provide the employee with specific feedback, and

   ◦ Document your actions.

Chapter 6
Best Practices in Performance Feedback

A strong supervisor-employee relationship leads to collaborative communication; collaborative communication supports successful feedback conversations.

Employee feedback isn't a luxury. It lets employees know whether or not they're on target in meeting expectations. It also helps you determine support needs, provide recognition, and hold employees accountable.

SUPPORTIVE ACCOUNTABILITY LEADERSHIP™

Unfortunately, as vital as feedback is to promoting strong performance, not all supervisors get it right. In the last two decades, I have seen managers and supervisors not prioritize this important element of performance management. Some implemented feedback haphazardly. Some didn't give feedback at all. Others limited their comments to sending employees a series of emails pointing out what they were doing wrong. They didn't recognize that effective feedback involves a two-way conversation. The goal isn't to point out performance concerns but to understand the employee's perspective, challenges, and needs so you can provide the support necessary for success. This requires dialogue—lots of it.

In other cases, leaders limited their feedback to the annual employee performance review, and this could hardly be called feedback. By the time you reach the performance review stage, it's too late to give the employee an opportunity to improve. If you're serious about positively impacting employee performance, limiting feedback to the performance review isn't enough.

Continuous Positive Feedback

Provide continuous positive feedback to employees in the form of appreciation, praise, and recognition when they're doing well in their regular job duties, not just when they're going above and beyond expectations. Continuous positive feedback lets employees know you're pleased with their performance and motivates them to continue on the same path.

Employees who don't receive frequent positive feedback may react in different ways. Those who feel safe and are more proactive may ask you directly how they're doing. Unfortunately, those who either don't feel safe or are less assertive may not ask for feedback.[47] They may begin to feel unappreciated, doubt their competence, or lose self-confidence. They may become dissatisfied, experience a dip in performance, and even leave your organization to work where they will feel appreciated. To keep employees motivated and engaged in their work, give them continuous positive feedback.

Early Intervention

Provide constructive feedback in a timely and proactive manner. I have seen managers and supervisors do well in monitoring and documenting issues, yet not provide timely feedback. They review performance data and conduct informal observations. Some make mental notes about their concerns and others diligently file the information. The problem is that they don't share the information with the employee. Some put off addressing concerns until the next recurring individual conference. Others don't address issues at all. Unfortunately, by delaying feedback, these leaders are not giving employees the opportunity to get it right. Even worse, as problems escalate, some leaders become frustrated and offload all their concerns in one sitting on the unsuspecting employee. Sometimes they don't reveal their concerns until the performance review, much to the employee's surprise. Not only are these approaches unfair and demoralizing, but they can trigger an adverse reaction from the employee and can destroy employee trust.

As a supervisor, engage in early intervention. As soon as employees veer off in the wrong direction, provide feedback. The sooner you intervene, the easier you make it for them to adjust. Waiting too long could result in employees forming undesirable habits which can be difficult to break. If you delay, today's small performance concern can end up being tomorrow's huge problem, which will then require much more time and energy to address. Also, ignoring performance difficulties and allowing them to escalate is neither the fair nor the caring thing to do.

Positive Approach

Use a positive approach that's supportive, meaningful, and constructive. Feedback isn't an opportunity to criticize employees for everything they have done wrong. This isn't a suggestion that you ignore performance shortcomings, but rather that you help employees leverage their strengths to improve performance. When you intentionally look for people's talent, skills, and passion, you set them up for success. Successful individuals make up successful teams, and successful teams make up successful organizations.

Using a positive approach to provide constructive feedback can strengthen performance and build trust. Employees will quickly realize that you have their backs, and they will have yours. Focusing the conversation solely on what employees are doing wrong will create distrust and put them on the defense. The walls will quickly go up, which will hinder receptiveness to feedback. This diminishes your ability to provide support and to inspire. A positive approach, even in difficult feedback conversations, yields better results.

Balanced Feedback

Provide balanced feedback. Discuss what the employee is doing well and what he needs to improve.

Some managers and supervisors struggle with corrective feedback. They find it easy to share "feel-good" information. However, they're apprehensive about engaging in performance improvement dialogue. This can stem from a variety of reasons, such as being uncomfortable with conflict, fear of negative employee reactions, lack of skill or self-confidence, and feeling overwhelmed. Whatever the reason, they don't provide employees with the input necessary to improve performance. This can lead to supportive unaccountability, where leaders worry too much about being liked and have difficulty holding themselves and their employees accountable.

Unfortunately, the reverse is also true. Some managers and supervisors relish the prospect of "getting" an employee during the feedback conversation. This "gotcha" approach to feedback is unsupportive accountability, where leaders operate with a high degree of accountability but fail to provide employees the support they need to succeed. The reasons for this type of feedback can vary, from an unhealthy desire to assert their power to lacking the necessary knowledge and skill to provide genuine, healthy, and supportive feedback. There may also be other underlying causes. Whatever the reason, this approach to feedback is unhealthy and damaging to the supervisor-employee relationship. Effective feedback builds the employee's self-awareness, self-confidence, and competence. Harsh feedback can't accomplish this.

For feedback to be at its most effective, provide it with the balanced approach of supportive accountability. Gauge each situation on a case-by-case basis and determine the levels of support and accountability the employee needs to be successful.

Collaborative Communication

Collaborative communication engages employees at the individual and group level in making decisions and finding solutions to concerns. No matter how experienced, intelligent, and efficient you are, you don't have all the answers. When you involve others in problem-solving efforts, you send a message that they have something valuable to offer and that their input matters. You also promote an environment of open dialogue and mutual learning that increases employee engagement.

Effective performance feedback involves two-way communication. Two-way conversation allows employees to communicate their expectations, feelings, successes, needs, and concerns. It also provides them with a forum to share openly and safely, which strengthens the supervisor-employee relationship, the foundation of supportive accountability. This creates what I call the Cycle of Collaborative Feedback. In this cycle, a strong supervisor-employee relationship leads to collaborative communication; collaborative communication supports successful feedback conversations; successful feedback conversations strengthen the supervisor-employee relationship; and the cycle continues.

The Cycle of Collaborative Feedback

Strong Supervisor-Employee Relationship

Collaborative Communication

Successful Feedback Conversations

Since collaborative feedback involves two-way communication, be proactive in asking employees what they need from you to be successful. This question rules out assumptions and provides employees the opportunity to voice any need whatsoever. This question tells employees they're valued and that you care. It helps you understand what employees need to perform with excellence.

Getting Personal

Some managers and supervisors believe that employees must leave their personal lives at home. Unfortunately, this doesn't work. We're holistic beings, and our professional and personal lives are interconnected. We can fool ourselves into thinking we can leave our personal problems at home, but we carry them with us, even if only subconsciously.

Because of this, collaborative feedback can get personal. You're working with people and not machines; therefore, feedback conversations should address the needs of the whole person on a physical, emotional, social, and psychological level. As you discuss the technical aspects of performance, you will also learn about employees' personal and professional needs, priorities, hopes, dreams, fears, and concerns.

Throughout the years, I have heard many heart-wrenching stories from my direct and indirect reports about their struggles with homelessness, mental health, physical health, finances, addictions, and other issues. They felt safe enough to trust me with this information. Sometimes, they just wanted me to listen, not to fix their problems. At other times, they were asking for help and looking for hope. In either case, I knew my responsibility was to provide them with support and resources. Sometimes this required that I admit these needs were beyond my level of expertise and reach out to my immediate manager or human resources. As a leader, employees need the same from you.

Be open to listening to your employees' personal problems if they choose to share them with you. There's a fine line between listening and prying, so be careful not to cross it. If employees volunteer personal information, then your role is to listen and to provide support. You're not their counselor, their doctor, their social worker, their psychologist, or their spiritual leader. However, you're responsible for knowing about the resources your organization either sponsors or endorses to assist employees in their time of need. Keep your manager and human resources informed of any serious support needs, such as those related to addictions, mental health, physical health, housing, and the like. They can inform you about available resources and your organization's protocol in addressing sensitive situations.

Focusing on Expectations and Results

Focus your feedback conversations on the employee's performance based on established goals and expectations and with the intention of teaching and developing. Discuss the employee's performance expectations and progress in achieving these. Share your thoughts on what you discovered during your monitoring activities. As much as possible, give concrete data and examples. Providing specific information helps the employee understand the information, self-reflect, and learn from the feedback experience. Emphasize how much growth the employee has already achieved. If there's room for additional growth and improvement, ask the employee for input on how she will accomplish this. Your role is to facilitate the employee's self-reflection and involve her in setting goals for her development, not to dictate the course of action. Empowering the employee to create her own path forward promotes autonomy, ownership, and pride.

Safeguarding Privacy

Hold performance feedback conversations in a comfortable environment that provides both auditory and visual privacy. An uncomfortable or non-private setting will make the employee uneasy, negatively impact the quality of the conversation, and hinder the employee's receptiveness to feedback. Keep strict confidentiality and safeguard the employee's privacy.

The Fishbowl

YouthZone was located on the first floor of a modern office building. The space had contemporary features, including a large conference room with beautiful glass walls. For this reason, employees jokingly called it "the fishbowl."

On the upside, the glass walls provided a feeling of openness and made the room look bigger. Natural light saturated the office and reached the people inside the glass conference room. This created an uplifting environment conducive to creativity. The glass walls also promoted transparency, which aligned with one of the core values of YouthZone. The people on the work floor could see those inside the conference room and vice versa. This naturally promoted accountability on both sides of the glass walls.

On the downside, the glass walls meant no visual privacy. Everyone on the work floor could see inside the conference room. Those walking by were immediately drawn into the action within the glass walls. They couldn't help but look inside. Because all eyes were continuously on those inside the fishbowl, the people outside were keenly tuned in to body language, the subtle and the not so subtle. Although they couldn't distinctly hear the dialogue going on inside, they could easily discern difficult conversations based on the facial expressions and body movements of the people within.

Alex was well aware of this lack of visual privacy in the conference room, so she asked Vic not to use it for his feedback conversation with Mary. She knew the fishbowl conditions created by the glass walls would make Mary feel uncomfortable, distract her, and compromise her privacy. Alex didn't want to put Mary on exhibition for all to see.

Therefore, Alex asked Vic to use the huddle room with normal walls that shielded its guests from spectators. Yes, it was much smaller than the fishbowl and certainly not as beautiful, but it was comfortable and private. And that's all that was needed.

Feedback Variety

Provide various forms of feedback in group and individual settings. Below are various ways you can provide feedback.

Team Performance Huddles

Team performance huddles are quick team meetings usually lasting no more than 15 to 30 minutes. They're an effective way to create a performance-oriented work culture and encourage team-level collaborative feedback. Use team performance huddles to provide performance updates, review performance goals and team progress, discuss obstacles, determine team support needs, and make team decisions to drive performance. To keep team huddles short, stay focused on a key performance topic or issue. A formal agenda isn't necessary. However, write down key points to keep these short meetings on track and within the allotted time.

As much as possible, schedule team performance huddles in advance. While these unplanned, short meetings are an effective way to mobilize your team, they can also be disruptive. Therefore, before holding an impromptu team huddle, carefully consider if it's necessary to get the job done. If the information isn't critical or time-sensitive or doesn't require face-to-face interaction, then it's best to use another vehicle to accomplish your goal. This can include emailing the information, folding it into an existing team meeting, or scheduling a separate meeting to address the issue. However, if a performance issue is time-sensitive or urgent, it warrants disruption.

Team Meetings

Hold regularly scheduled team meetings at a minimum on a monthly basis. Calendar these meetings at least twelve months in advance, use a structured agenda, and share it with team members before each meeting. This will allow team members to come prepared and will make your team meetings more productive. These recurring meetings don't have to cover just performance. However, add a recurring agenda item about performance goals and objectives, as well as team progress, to keep employees focused on what matters.

Staff Meetings

If you manage a large program or office, hold regularly scheduled staff meetings for your entire workforce to share the bigger picture. Use this forum to reinforce the organization's overarching vision and to provide updates on key performance goals and group progress in achieving these goals. Have an agenda to stay focused and on track. The frequency of these meetings will depend on the size of your workforce, the facilities available to you, and the nature of your work.

I once managed a workforce of a few hundred employees and consistently conducted monthly staff meetings. Although the group was rather large, the staff was located in the same building, we had a sizeable multipurpose conference room, and we operated in a dynamic environment that required continuous communication. Given the size of the workforce, we held the meeting in two sessions, one in the morning and one in the afternoon. This made the meeting more manageable and minimized disruption to our operations.

Individual On-the-Spot Feedback

Individual on-the-spot feedback can be verbal or written. However, be careful when providing corrective feedback via email. Although it's quick and easy, it can harm your supervisor-employee relationship depending on how much correction is needed. If you need to give a gentle reminder, then email may be an appropriate vehicle. However, if the concern is significant or requires a lengthy explanation, it's better to provide in-person feedback instead. Email isn't a useful vehicle for comprehensive feedback. Employees may misinterpret intention and tone in an email. If you find yourself going back and forth with an employee via email with no resolution, it's time to have a conversation.

Individual Unplanned Check-ins

Unplanned check-ins should range from a few minutes to about half an hour, depending on the nature of the topic and the amount of guidance and decision-making required. If your unplanned check-ins are taking more than 30 minutes, you may need to schedule status check meetings or individual conferences instead. Nevertheless, the value of these impromptu conversations can't be underscored enough. They will help you obtain real-time information and keep your finger on the pulse of how the employee is doing. These informal conversations build rapport and promote a strong supervisor-employee relationship. They help you establish trust, provide adequate guidance, and nurture a cooperative working relationship. Employees will begin to feel free and safe to share their thoughts. This will give you a realistic picture of what is going on with your team and individual employees.

Status Check Meetings

When you assign a new role or project to an employee, set up periodic status check meetings. If the project is of high importance and visibility, meet with the employee more frequently. As soon as you make the assignment, let the employee know you will be meeting with him regularly to receive updates on how things are going. These meetings are your opportunity to assess the employee's progress, identify challenges, and provide the necessary support to meet project goals. Clarify the information or data he needs to prepare ahead of time. Be as specific as possible so that he doesn't have to guess what you need. What you request may vary depending on the project or assignment. Let the employee know if you require regular written updates, the information he should provide, the format you prefer, and the delivery frequency. The more clarity you offer, the more you equip the employee to meet your expectations.

Recurring Individual Conferences

Recurring individual employee conferences help you develop a habit of continuous, regular feedback. Hold these conferences at least once a month. If the employee is new, on probation, or struggling, you can increase the frequency of these regular feedback sessions to biweekly or even weekly. However, if the employee requires excessive supervisory intervention, keep your manager and human resources informed. The earlier you seek guidance in the performance management process, the earlier they can assist you in achieving a successful outcome. Also, the sooner you let them know about the difficulties, the less likely they will be surprised if they escalate. You don't want to surprise your manager or human resources.

Schedule recurring individual conferences with ample notice to employees. Invite them to meet with you to discuss their successes, challenges, and support needs. These regularly scheduled meetings are an opportunity for you to build and reinforce positive supervisor-employee relationships through supportive accountability. Employees report on their progress in meeting expectations, and you render an account on the provision of support.

Recurring individual conferences are not for you to have difficult conversations about performance issues, but occasionally, due to timing, you may need to use these conferences to address concerns. If this is the case, be candid. However, don't accumulate all your concerns about an employee's performance or behavior and unload them all during your recurring individual conference. This can be demoralizing for the employee. He may become overwhelmed with too much negative feedback at one time. Feeling attacked, he may become defensive, which hinders his ability to listen, self-reflect, and learn. If this happens, he will walk away from the conversation feeling beat up, unappreciated, misunderstood, or even picked on. This is detrimental to his self-confidence, motivation, performance, engagement, and commitment to your organization.

Using recurring individual conferences to unload concerns creates uncertainty for employees, as they won't know what to expect during these important meetings. This may cause them to approach these conferences in a guarded manner, which isn't conducive to trust, honesty, and collaborative communication. Instead, use these recurring appointments to strengthen your relationships. Employees will then look forward to their conferences expecting to receive the support and guidance necessary to succeed.

Performance Improvement Conversations

If you need to discuss performance concerns with employees, do so in an individual performance improvement conversation scheduled explicitly for this purpose. More information about this type of feedback is available in Chapter 7, "Leading Performance Improvement Conversations."

Documentation Tip: Document individual feedback conversations using a Conversation Notes Template (Appendix K), a Manual Event Log (Appendix L), an Electronic Event Log (Appendix M), or another format. File a copy of this documentation in the employee's file.

In Review

Feedback is an essential form of support. When done correctly, it lets employees know if they're on the right track in meeting expectations and helps you identify and provide the support they need to succeed. Provide continuous positive feedback and intervene as soon as employees start to veer off course. Use a positive and balanced feedback approach of supportive accountability that engages the employee and promotes collaboration. Because employees are people, feedback often gets personal, and employees reveal their private lives. To encourage a strong supervisor-employee relationship, embrace this. However, focus your feedback conversations on established performance expectations and results. Finally, hold feedback conversations in a comfortable space that safeguards employee privacy and use a variety of ways to provide feedback, both at the group and individual levels.

Putting It into Action

1. Schedule monthly individual conferences with your direct reports. Increase the frequency as needed by each employee.

2. Schedule monthly unit meetings with your team.

3. If you manage a large program, office, or section, schedule monthly staff meetings.

Chapter 7
Leading Performance Improvement Conversations

When provided through a collaborative, two-way conversation,
performance improvement feedback is a critical support factor.

As a leader, providing employees with the support and account-ability they need to succeed is your most important responsibility. When offered through a collaborative, two-way conversation, perfor-mance improvement feedback is a critical support factor. It's also a tool that helps you uncover the specific support employees need to improve their performance.

SUPPORTIVE ACCOUNTABILITY LEADERSHIP™

Performance improvement conversations are often the most difficult to have with employees. Letting employees know that they're not performing at expected levels can be awkward and stressful. But it doesn't have to be that way. You can have performance improvement conversations without the angst.

10 Keys to Effective Performance Improvement Conversations

There are 10 keys you can apply to your performance improvement conversations to reduce anxiety.

Key 1 – Immediacy

Hold performance improvement conversations immediately following the discovery of difficulties. If the concerns involve an incident, the events will still be fresh in people's minds. Immediate feedback allows the employee to correct issues quickly and prevent escalation. When you delay feedback, you're nonverbally approving of unacceptable performance and behavior. Your silence and inaction are detrimental to your organization's work culture. You have a responsibility to promote accountability.

Key 2 – Timing

Some circumstances may require that you wait for better timing before having performance improvement conversations. These circumstances can range from the purely logistical to those involving various levels of sensitivity. Here are just a few examples:

- The employee suffered an unfortunate event just before your scheduled meeting. This could include a death in the family, an injury, the diagnosis of a serious illness, or another unexpected incident taking an emotional toll on the employee.

- You work in a unionized environment, and the issue you're addressing is the subject of labor negotiations.

- The issue you're addressing is tied to an investigation, and you must wait for the results before proceeding.

- The employee filed a grievance or complaint shortly before the performance issue came to light. The timing can give the employee the erroneous impression that the performance improvement conversation is in retaliation.

It's important to be aware of sensitivities that could affect timing, but these don't relieve you of the responsibility of addressing performance issues. Work closely with your manager and human resources to ensure your timing is appropriate.

Key 3 – Honesty

To gain and maintain your employee's trust, be as honest and transparent as appropriate. Don't sugarcoat or minimize the issue. It's disconcerting to employees when supervisors have lighthearted conversations with them, then issue a written warning or add unfavorable language to their performance evaluations. If an issue is serious, be candid about it. Employees may not always like or agree with your feedback, but they will appreciate that you speak the truth. They don't have to guess how they're performing because you consistently let them know with honesty and transparency.

Key 4 – No Assumptions

Don't make assumptions about the causes of poor performance or speculate about the employee's intentions. Assumptions have a dangerous way of tainting your perspective and undermining objectivity. Sure, you may have some preliminary thoughts on the situation based on the information you have already gathered. However, give the employee an opportunity to share his side of the story to get the complete picture. Gather all the pertinent facts before arriving at conclusions.

Key 5 – Focus

When possible, focus performance improvement feedback on one overarching issue or area of concern. If you address concerns as soon as they arise, they won't accumulate. Overwhelming the employee with too many problems at once will make it difficult for him to focus on the most pressing issue at hand. If you have multiple unrelated concerns, consider prioritizing them in order of impact, severity, and urgency and concentrating on the most pressing issue first. Then systematically focus on the others. However, there may be exceptions, and you will need to exercise sound judgment. Your manager and human resources can help you determine the best approach.

Key 6 – Expectations

Base performance improvement conversations on expectations you have already communicated. You can't hold the employee accountable for meeting expectations you haven't expressed. Provide concrete examples of how the employee isn't meeting established standards and what she needs to accomplish to be successful. Use the information from your performance monitoring activities as a springboard for conversation.

Key 7 – Support

Assess the employee's support needs. Ask him what he needs from you to be successful. Does he need tools, training, or equipment? Or does he simply need more autonomy? Sometimes employees actually need a little less of you.

If the employee doesn't have the necessary support to meet expectations, it will hinder performance. Honor the employee's support requests as much as reasonably possible. If any of the requests are unfeasible, explain why so he knows you considered them. Neglecting to honor support requests without explanation will negatively affect the employee's trust in you. Your responsibility is to set the employee up for success by providing the necessary support. His responsibility is to use the support to achieve success.

Key 8 – Agility

There's no script for effective performance improvement feedback. If you try to use one, you may end up frustrated when the employee deviates from it. Tailor your approach to each unique situation and individual. Plan for the performance improvement conversation, but be agile and keep in mind that the employee's responses or reactions may require you to shift gears quickly. Don't go into the discussion expecting for it to go 100% as planned. It seldom does.

Key 9 – Preparation

If the conversation is serious or you must issue something in writing, try to schedule the meeting towards the end of the employee's work shift. Should the employee experience a negative reaction to the conversation, you can offer the option of going home early. If the employee doesn't feel well after the interaction, he may not be able to focus on his work and his judgment, productivity, customer service, and other performance areas may be adversely affected. If you're unable to schedule a meeting later in the employee's shift, offer the employee a few minutes to go outside and get a breath of fresh air before returning to work. However, the employee may still need to go home early, depending on how he feels.

Have facial tissue on hand in case the employee cries or sweats during the conversation. Your approach should be one of supportive accountability; however, it's hard to predict how performance improvement conversations will turn out. Even if you think the chat will be casual, the employee's reaction may be different than anticipated.

Documentation Tip: Refer to Appendix J – Performance Improvement Conversation Plan for an example of how to prepare.

Key 10 – Seeking Guidance

Before you have performance improvement conversations, share your planned approach with your manager and human resources. Write down a brief outline of the topics and facts you plan to cover and what you intend to say. If your organization has an employee union, ask your manager or human resources whether a union representative must be present during the conversation. Also, ask about your organization's procedures for union involvement. Should your manager or human resources participate in the conference if a union representative is present? How much notice do you need to give the employee about the meeting? Are there any other steps you need to take?

These ten keys will help you set the stage for effective performance improvement conversations. Now let's review the steps you need to take for these conversations to yield positive results.

Seven Steps for Collaborative Performance Improvement Conversations

These seven steps can help you facilitate collaborative performance improvement conversations.

Step 1 – Start the conversation on a positive note.

The opening sets the tone for the rest of the conversation. Starting on a positive note will help you establish rapport from the onset.

Step 2 – Explain the purpose of the conversation.

Let the employee know that the meeting is to review the employee's performance and to identify her support needs.

Step 3 – Review the employee's performance.

Provide specific examples of how the employee is performing relative to the performance goal.

Step 4 – Ask for the employee's perspective and input.

Ask various questions to get the employee's perspective and input. What are the employee's successes? Challenges? Struggles? What help does the employee need to be successful? You can modify these questions. The point is to ask questions and listen carefully to the employee's responses, as these will shed light on what you can do to provide support. Sometimes the employee may ask for support you think she doesn't need. However, what matters is what the employee believes she needs.

Even if you don't agree with the employee's request, if it doesn't create a major burden for you and the organization, grant it. It will be a win-win. She will feel heard, supported, and empowered. This act of good faith will demonstrate that you care about the employee's success, and you will gain her trust.

Step 5 – Provide feedback and guidance.

Provide the employee with feedback on her self-assessment and performance. If the employee doesn't realize she needs improvement, guide her through self-reflection. Help her come up with ideas on how to improve her performance. Share some examples of best practices. Encourage her throughout the process, and use an approach that's positive and supportive.

Step 6 –Reach an agreement.

Reach an agreement with the employee regarding the support you will provide and the actions she will take to improve performance. Establish measurable goals for improvement that the two of you can use to evaluate progress.

Step 7 – Set a follow-up meeting.

Establish a date and time for you and the employee to meet again to discuss the support you provided and to review her progress.

These seven steps establish an overall framework for having effective performance improvement conversations. However, employees don't follow a formula, script, or sequence. Be prepared to adapt these steps to the employee's responses. Agility is paramount. The key is to use each step to establish a strong foundation for performance improvement.

Vic Meets with Mary

Vic had reviewed Mary's Customer Satisfaction Report, conducted observations of Mary's interactions, and consulted with Alex. Now he was sitting at the small table in the middle of the huddle room, waiting for Mary to arrive for their performance improvement conversation. Vic sat facing the open door. He was staring at the clock. Tick tock. Tick tock.

Vic was nervous. He had been a supervisor for two years, but he had never discussed any type of performance issues before. In the past, he had supervised a couple of counselors who didn't pull their weight, but Vic had managed to get his star performers to help him keep up his numbers.

Mary was now at the door. There was no turning back.

"Hi, Mary. Come in and have a seat." Vic gestured to the table in the middle of the small huddle room, his voice a little shaky. As

Mary walked towards the table and sat down, Vic caught her staring at the folder on the table. His heart was beating fast, and his palms were sweaty.

Yes, Vic was definitely nervous. But he couldn't let on how he felt. He had to look confident. And why shouldn't he be? He had followed all of Alex's instructions. He had his facts together, and he had rehearsed several times what he would say. What more could he have possibly done to prepare?

Vic cleared his throat. "I asked you to meet with me so we could discuss your customer service."

Vic opened the folder. Mary's eyes followed Vic's hands. Vic ruffled through the papers, took out two reports, and handed one to Mary.

"I know you're aware that Alex implemented a customer satisfaction program a couple of months ago," Vic said.

"Yes, you mentioned it to us during our team meeting," acknowledged Mary.

"Well," Vic continued, "as part of the new program, one of our new performance goals is to achieve an average customer satisfaction rating of 4 or higher in all areas measured by the customer satisfaction surveys. Here's a copy of your Customer Satisfaction Report for May."

Mary flipped through the pages of her Employee Customer Satisfaction Report. Stapled neatly behind the report were copies of the supporting customer satisfaction surveys.

Vic said, "Five of your customers submitted surveys last month. As you can see, your ratings were great in the areas of promptness and assistance. You're serving your customers quickly and providing them what they need, which are both important to their success. Unfortunately, your scores were low in the other two areas, professionalism and responsiveness."

Vic asked, "What are your thoughts about your scores?"

Mary shrugged her shoulders.

Vic elaborated. "Your average rating in responsiveness was 3.8, which…uh…didn't meet the goal of 4 or higher. For professionalism, it was only 2.6. This is really low." There was a momentary awkwardness. "So…I was wondering if you had any ideas of what may be causing the low scores."

"No, I don't," Mary answered with a bite in her voice. Her arms were crossed and her face looked tense.

Vic could feel his heart pounding against his chest. He took a deep breath and continued as he had rehearsed. "Let's take a closer look at the report. If you notice, your lowest score was in professionalism. Unfortunately, of the four youth that rated you low in professionalism, only one provided comments. And the only thing the comment said is that you were rude."

"Me, rude?" Mary asked. "How am I rude? I work hard to serve these kids. I get them placed in jobs as quickly as I can. I can't help it if they have bad attitudes and feel like the world owes them." Mary was agitated.

Vic responded, "You certainly get your work done timely. The performance reports show that. And, based on their responses to the surveys, the teens agree. They gave you an average rating of 4.6 for promptness."

After this acknowledgment, Vic redirected Mary to the discussion at hand. "But that's not what we're talking about now. We're talking about professionalism. And the youth feel that you're not treating them professionally. They feel that you're rude to them."

"Well, what am I supposed to do? I don't know what these kids want from me," Mary said in frustration.

Vic answered, "I had the same question. Unfortunately, the surveys don't contain much detail, and none of the teens wanted to be contacted. That's why I observed three of your customer interactions last week. Remember?"

"Yeah, I remember," said Mary.

"These observations provided some good information, which I think you might find helpful," Vic said.

"So what did you find?" Mary asked.

Vic shared the findings of his observations. At first, it was uncomfortable for him. But the more they talked, the more he felt at ease.

Vic couldn't get Mary to say much, so he shared his thoughts about how Mary could improve her customer service. He acknowledged Mary's speed in getting the work done. However, he also pointed out that in her haste to work quickly, she was neither listening to nor establishing rapport with her customers and was coming across as rude.

Vic also shared the complaint letter Alex had received.

Vic clarified that Mary was expected to approach customer interactions with professionalism, which included courtesy and respect. He gave a few examples and tips. Mary reluctantly agreed to take more time with her interactions and to listen more to her customers.

Vic set up a follow-up meeting with Mary to review her progress.

Documentation Tip: Immediately following performance improvement conversations, document them. Provide copies to your manager and human resources, following your organization's protocol, and retain copies of what you submitted.

Progressive Discipline Conversations

When an issue is serious or continues to recur in spite of consistent feedback and support, you may need to continue on the progressive discipline path. Chapter 11, "Boosting Performance through Progressive Discipline," provides more information.

The Cost of Avoidance

Nothing hurts the morale of employees more than a supervisor who doesn't hold all employees equally accountable. The cost of avoidance is threefold. First, it impacts the morale of other employees, which in turn can affect their engagement and performance. Second, it enables struggling employees to continue with poor performance and does nothing to help them improve. Third, it takes a toll on the performance of your team and your organization. Performance improvement feedback is one of the hardest things for many supervisors to do. Yet, avoidance will hurt your customers, your team, and your organization.

The Board Complaint

It was June 28th. Vic was crunching numbers, trying to project what his team's performance in job placement and retention would be by the end of the month. It looked like it would be another great month.

He heard a faint alert coming from his computer. It was the familiar sound of an email hitting his inbox. He clicked on his inbox and there it was, an email from Alex. It read, "Vic, please see the email below from one of our board members. He received a complaint about Mary. You have to get this under control. Please come to my office."

Vic rushed to Alex's office. After an extensive conversation with Alex and YouthZone's HR manager, he walked back to his office, wearing a serious look on his face. They had asked him to meet with Mary, but not now. They wanted him to wait until he had the full Customer Satisfaction Report for June, which wouldn't be available until July 1st. The HR manager didn't want Vic to meet with Mary now about the board complaint, then have another meeting with her after the June report was available in a few days. The HR manager preferred that he discuss her customer service issues in one sitting.

Alex and the HR manager scheduled a meeting with Vic on July 2nd to help him prepare for this next conversation with Mary. They instructed Vic to print, review, and bring a copy of the June report to this meeting, where they would both coach him on how to approach the upcoming conversation with Mary.

This was all he needed. Mary had caused an escalation to Youth-Zone's board of directors, and now Alex and HR were both on him. He definitely needed to get this under control. It was a big time waster.

Mastering Performance Improvement Feedback

Performance improvement feedback is an art and a mission-critical skill. As a supervisor, you must master the art of effective performance feedback. This comes through proper training and practice. Take advantage of the training offered directly by your organization. This training should be tailored to your organization's mission, vision, values, and culture. Avail yourself of other resources, such as books and additional training that focus on using a positive approach to employee feedback. Above all, practice. The better you get at providing employee feedback, both positive and corrective, the more you're going to make a positive impact on your team's and your organization's performance.

In Review

Performance improvement feedback provided in a spirit of supportive accountability is a critical support factor and a tool that helps you determine the support needs of employees. You can facilitate effective performance improvement conversations by applying ten key principles:

1. Immediacy

2. Timing

3. Honesty

4. No assumptions

5. Focus

6. Expectations

7. Support

8. Agility

9. Preparation

10. Guidance seeking

These ten keys lay a strong foundation for you to carry out the seven steps for collaborative performance improvement conversations. These seven steps are:

1. Start the conversation on a positive note.

2. Explain the purpose of the conversation.

3. Review the employee's performance.

4. Ask for the employee's perspective and input.

5. Provide feedback and guidance.

6. Reach an agreement.

7. Set a follow-up meeting.

Performance improvement conversations are often the most difficult to have with employees. However, the cost of avoiding these difficult conversations is high. It impacts the morale of the other employees, who either have to pick up the slack of co-workers who are underperforming or who view the workplace as unfair because of the lack of accountability. It also enables underperforming employees to continue performing poorly and doesn't provide them with the necessary support and guidance to succeed. Performance improvement conversations, when done correctly, are not punitive. They're part of the support role that you as a supervisor must skillfully play for the success of employees.

Putting It into Action

1. Before having your next performance improvement conversation, take the time to prepare your approach. Sometimes it's helpful to write out your plan ahead of time.

2. Take responsibility for your own development needs. Could you use additional training and practice in leading effective performance improvement conversations? If yes, what online and in-person training is available through your organization? Are there additional resources that can help you?

3. Talk to your supervisor about your development desires and needs.

Chapter 8
Critical Support Factors that Unleash Performance

"The area where individuals fall short is the support piece. It's maybe
tools, maybe software, or maybe leadership support. It could be that
there are no incentives in place for employees to do their job."

– Barbara Greenstein, Principal of Human Resources Prescriptions, LLC

It's not enough to provide clear expectations, monitor performance, and provide feedback. To perform at their best, employees need support.[48] You can't rely on employees telling you when they need assistance. You must establish a strong supervisor-employee relationship, continuously focus your team on meeting performance expectations, and ask them what they need to be successful.

DOCUMENTATION   EXPECTATIONS

ACCOUNTABILITY   SUPPORTIVE   MONITORING
ACCOUNTABILITY

RECOGNITION   FEEDBACK

SUPPORT

SUPPORTIVE ACCOUNTABILITY
LEADERSHIP™

113

It's impractical to provide an exhaustive list of all possible employee support needs. However, let's go over some critical support factors frequently identified in the workplace.

Tools, Equipment, and Supplies

All occupations require tools for work to be performed efficiently. Secretaries need computers, printers, telephone systems, and other office supplies to work effectively. Surgeons need surgical instruments such as clamps, retractors, and scalpels to perform their jobs with precision. Pilots depend heavily on flight instruments, such as airspeed indicators and altimeters, to safely navigate their aircraft. Janitors need adequate cleaning and disinfecting supplies that are appropriate for the specific cleaning job, from minor spills to biohazardous waste. In every job, lack of resources diminishes productivity, undermines performance, and increases employee frustration and stress.

Training

It's not enough to give employees the necessary tools, equipment, and supplies. Great leaders also ensure employees have the knowledge, skills, abilities, and mindset to use all the resources available to them. This is where training and development come in.

Training Can Improve Performance

Training, when implemented correctly, improves performance.[49] It prepares and inspires employees to take their performance, behavior, and mindset to the next level. It takes raw talent, refines it, and unleashes it in the workplace. It also builds, reinforces, and sustains a workplace culture that aligns with your organization's values and advances the vision. Training reinforces expectations. It teaches employees how to do their job and how to do it well. From the smallest tasks to the most complex projects and initiatives, the work employees do is ultimately about serving customers with excellence through great performance.

Establish a Training Schedule

Training is so essential for individual and organizational success that you must provide it on a regular basis,[50] from the time the employee first sets foot in the workplace and continuing throughout her career with your organization. Consider providing training at the following critical junctures:

- New-employee onboarding
- New task assignment
- New position or role
- Development
- Preparation for advancement
- Need for a new challenge
- Visible performance gaps or difficulties
- Need for mindset adjustment
- Need for behavior change
- Reinforcement of organizational expectations, values, or priorities

However, before you provide training, determine if it's an appropriate solution.

Training Doesn't Always Improve Performance

When appropriate, training can be an important part of the solution for employee performance improvement. Unfortunately, training in and of itself isn't always the answer. Effective performance improvement requires a targeted approach that focuses on the specific support needs of employees at the group and individual levels. The appropriate intervention, which is the result of an analysis process, may or may not include training.

I interviewed Barbara Greenstein, the principal of Human Resource Prescriptions, LLC, with regard to the issue.[51] Barbara is a performance improvement consultant with over 20 years of experience in learning and development and human performance improvement. She's an award-winning facilitator and a past adjunct professor for the master's program in human resource development at Brandman University in San Diego, California. She also facilitates certificate programs through the Association for Talent Development (ATD).

Barbara shared that the biggest pitfall she's seen in using training for employee performance improvement is that managers often train their entire workforce to correct one individual's performance problem. Barbara said, "It's one person, but they implement that program for everyone in that department, when everyone in that department doesn't have a problem. So that creates issues. That's a big pitfall."[52]

Barbara explained that managers often rationalize this mass training as a way of not singling out an individual. She underscored how prevalent and costly this is. She said, "I see it over and over again, no matter what the industry, no matter what the level in the organization. It's a knee-jerk reaction based on what they know and based on their past experience. It could easily be resolved differently, cost less, take less time, and most importantly be much more effective."[53]

Barbara described some of the issues that arise with using this type of blanket approach to training. First, unnecessary mass training has a negative impact on the morale of employees who don't need the training. Second, providing unnecessary training to an entire workforce, department, or team is very costly and wasteful. Third, by not working closely to support the individual who is struggling, managers and supervisors are not "able to fine-tune what that one person needs to be productive."[54]

More information about Barbara Greenstein and her company, Human Resources Prescriptions, LLC, is available at http://www. hrxi.com/team.php.

The bottom line is that training can be and often is a viable tool for performance improvement. However, it can't be your default reaction to solve all performance and behavioral problems in the workplace. Training is only effective when it springs out of a solid needs assessment.[55] If you determine in this assessment that the employee lacks the necessary knowledge, skills, abilities, and mindset to meet expectations, then training can be a part of the solution. However, if the root cause of the performance or behavioral issue rests elsewhere, training is a waste of time, energy, and money. Also, just because one employee may need additional training to meet expectations, it doesn't mean that training is appropriate for the entire workforce, department, or unit. That determination would require an assessment.

Employees Must Learn and Apply What They Learn

Training is successful only when employees learn and apply what they learn in the workplace.

As a leader, you play a vital support role in helping employees apply new knowledge gained through training. You must understand employees' motivation to learn and apply and communicate the benefits of learning and application.[56]

If you understand the motivation behind employees' desire to learn or lack thereof, you will be in a much better position to provide supportive accountability. Employees can be motivated to learn for a variety of reasons. These may include preparing for promotion, transferring to a different type of work, developing expertise, making more money, the mere love of learning, or other reasons. The motivation to learn is unique to each individual. When you get to know employees, you discover what gets them excited about learning and application.

Unfortunately, some individuals may have no interest in learning. Organizations often require mandated training that doesn't excite employees. This lack of interest can have several reasons, such as having too much work, viewing the training as a waste of time, or feeling that leadership is merely running employees through assembly line instruction to check it off a to-do list. Some employees may be dreaming of retirement, waiting to serve their remaining time with your organization. Others may have additional reasons.

When employees are not motivated to learn, and you send them to training, they will go through the motions so they can comply with the mandate. Their bodies will be present, but their minds will be absent. This negatively affects their engagement, their actual learning, and consequently their application. The stronger your supervisor-employee relationship is with each employee, the more you will understand their motivation to learn and apply.

There are several ways to encourage employees to practice what they learn.

Using Games in Training to Encourage Application

Barbara Greenstein facilitates a course through ATD called "Essentials of Game Design," where participants can learn how to develop games to enhance their training development. During our interview, Barbara shared that incorporating games into training is a way to help participants learn and immediately practice what they learn. Barbara said that games provide an experiential type of learning. They provide "a simulation of what might happen in the real world." Barbara explained, "Games are competitive, and they're a fast track to learning because people are engaged while they're doing them, and they're starting to incorporate the knowledge into their short-term memory. Then, as they're building their knowledge through the gaming activity, they're taking that information and starting to store it in their long-term memory. It's one of those methods that allows them to get the information into the long-term memory, so when they go back into the office, something happens. Something triggers it, and suddenly they pull it from their short-term memory and pull the other information from the long-term memory, and they start to make it happen in the workplace."[57]

Barbara makes a strong case for the value of selecting learning solutions for employees that are based on great design and incorporate activities and games that can engage, promote deeper levels of learning, and allow for immediate application of new knowledge. Long-winded lectures don't engage learners. As a leader, be selective about the quality of the training you provide employees.

The Supervisor's Role

Top-quality training isn't enough to help employees apply what they learn to achieve stronger performance. Ismail et al. emphasized the vital role direct supervisors play in encouraging application. The researchers wrote about the importance of "supervisors openly delivering information about the procedures, content, tasks and objectives of the training program, conducting discussions about tasks that should be learned, giving detailed explanations about the benefits of attending training programs and providing performance feedback." [58]

When you send an employee to training, clarify the purpose, whether it's to acquire new skills, prepare for advancement, earn a certification, improve performance, or another reason. Be honest. Explain the importance and benefits of attending the training, the expected outcomes, and how you will support the employee and hold him accountable for applying what he learned. Offer him the necessary time and space to implement the concepts. Follow up with the employee after training and ask exploratory questions. How did it go? What new insights did he learn? How has he leveraged the concepts? What roadblocks is the employee encountering in using his new knowledge, and what can you do to support him?

The Heart-to-Heart

It was the morning of July 5th, and Vic was once again sitting with Mary in the huddle room. He was well prepared. Alex and the HR manager had coached him on what to say and what not say. They had gone over several possible scenarios with him and had even forced him to do that ridiculous role-playing. Hopefully, it would pay off. He was ready to get this under control.

Vic opened the conversation with Mary. "The reason I asked you to meet with me is that I want to discuss your progress in the area of customer service. I pulled a copy of your Employee Customer Satisfaction Report for June."

It was like clockwork. He repeated the same drill he had gone through with Mary last month when they had reviewed May's report. And just like last month, Mary's responses were limited and unhelpful. Still, Vic went over the report in depth. Again, her scores in professionalism and responsiveness were below expected levels.

"In addition to you not meeting customer satisfaction expectations, Alex recently received a complaint about your customer service. Unfortunately, this complaint came through the board of directors."

Vic explained the details of the complaint and asked if Mary had any questions. She didn't.

"Mary, this can't continue," Vic emphasized. "You're a great worker and a high performer, but you have to turn your customer service around. You can't continue to get low customer satisfaction ratings, and you can't continue to get complaints. How can I help you turn this around?"

Mary shrugged her shoulders.

"Is there anything you can think of that can help?" Vic asked.

"I don't know what these kids expect from me, Vic," Mary grumbled. "I work hard every day. I don't know what else I can do. And I don't feel I'm rude."

"Unfortunately, our customers don't agree with you, Mary," Vic rebutted. "They feel you treat them disrespectfully. If this were only one teen's perception, it wouldn't be as concerning. But several teens have reported that they feel disrespected by you. And remember that last month I conducted observations of three of your interactions with your customers? I shared my findings with you. You had areas you could improve on. I even gave you some tips. This is a pattern, and now it's up to you to make some changes."

"Well, I don't know what you want me to change," Mary objected.

"Okay. So maybe I can help clarify that," Vic responded. "Great customer service is a skill. And there are techniques you can use to help our teens feel valued and respected. Here's some information about a two-hour, online customer service training that will go over these techniques." Vic handed Mary a computer printout describing the online training. "Please complete the training in the next three days. By the end of today, please enroll and let me know what date and time you'll be taking the training. I'll have the clerk reschedule any of your appointments that conflict with your training."

Vic also handed Mary a small, hardcover notebook. "I also got you this journal. As you take the training, please use it to take notes. Write down at least two to three techniques you learned from the training and how you plan to apply them in your interactions with your customers. Do you have any questions so far?"

No response. Mary looked tense.

Vic felt awkward, but he put on his confident face and pressed on. "After you complete the training, please start applying these techniques in your customer interactions. Following these interactions, please reflect and write down your thoughts in your journal. You can write about the techniques you applied and how the interaction went. Do have any questions about this portion of your learning process?"

"This seems like a lot of work, and I'm busy trying to meet your numbers." Mary balked. "How am I supposed to do that and all this journaling at the same time?"

Vic countered. "I understand how you feel. I feel the same way. This is going to take a lot of time and work from both of us. But you have to turn your customer service around. We talked about this last month, and here we are again. And you said that you don't know what you need to do. So you taking this online training, journaling, and sharing your progress with me will help you figure that out. Now the sooner you turn this around, the sooner you and I don't have to keep doing this, and we can focus on our work. It's all up to you." Vic put the ball back in Mary's court.

Mary didn't respond.

Emboldened, Vic said, "The expectation is that you apply the techniques from the training and use your journal to self-reflect, so you can stop receiving complaints from your customers and can start meeting the goal of an average customer satisfaction rating of 4 or higher on your Monthly Customer Satisfaction Report. Do you understand these expectations?"

"Yes," Mary grumbled.

Vic added, "The other thing I wanted to let you know is that when a customer submits a customer satisfaction survey, I am alerted right away by our new survey software." He then confessed, "I haven't been sharing these with you as I get them, and I'm sorry about that." Taking responsibility for not sharing customer complaints with Mary early on was difficult for Vic. But he had to do it. He knew he needed to admit that he had some room for improvement too.

Vic assured Mary, "I really want you to be successful. I am going to start sharing the surveys with you right away, so you can use the customer feedback as part of your self-reflection and learning. I'm also scheduling a follow-up meeting for us one month from now so you can share what you wrote in your journal and we can review your progress. I'll send you the invitation right after this meeting."

"Fine," Mary sneered.

Vic gave the final and most awkward piece of information. "One more thing. I am going to put this conversation in writing, summarizing what we discussed to be sure we're both on the same page. We have talked about this before. Yet, your customer satisfaction ratings haven't improved, and you had a second complaint elevated to the board of directors. It's important that you start turning this around. If you have any questions, concerns, or need anything from me to meet these expectations, please let me know."

By now, Mary was seething. Her eyes were glaring, and her eyebrows were pointing sharply towards the center of her face. But she was silent.

Vic cleared his throat. "Okay, Mary. Thank you for meeting with me. I look forward to the improvement."

Mary walked out without saying a word.

Access to Information

A big part of supporting employees is to ensure they have access to information. You don't need to overwhelm them with all the information in one sitting, but you do need to give them the tools to find the information they need. The information has to be user-friendly, well organized, and easy to retrieve. Below are a few tools you can use to provide access to information:

- Employee manuals, guides, handbooks, and informational brochures

- Employee newsletters
- Job aids and tip sheets
- Web-based resources
- Electronic and manual bulletin boards

Know where to find essential information and let employees know how to access it.

Employee Assistance Programs

As you establish strong supervisor-employee relationships, employees will begin to trust you and become vulnerable with you. As a result, they may share personal and sensitive information with you, including issues that may require extensive support and intervention. This can include information on substance abuse, mental health issues, addictions, or other sensitive information. For you to support them in the best way possible, you must know and understand the resources available to employees through your organization.

Many organizations offer Employee Assistance Programs (EAPs). The availability and structure of EAPs vary from organization to organization. These programs support employee well-being in areas such as physical health, mental health, freedom from addictions, and work/life balance.

EAPs can provide direct assistance to employees with issues such as mental illness, emotional challenges, drug and alcohol abuse, smoking cessation, divorce, parenting, elderly care, financial well-being, weight loss, career planning, legal support, and many more. EAPs can also help human resources professionals, managers, and supervisors in addressing challenging workplace situations. This may include help in supporting employees through hard times and in managing difficult environmental circumstances such as workplace violence, workforce reductions, and major transitions.[59]

EAPs are a valuable resource for the employee and the

organization. According to the U.S. Department of Labor, Office of Disability Employment Policy, "EAPs have been shown to contribute to decreased absenteeism, reduced accidents and fewer workers compensation claims, greater employee retention, fewer labor disputes, and significantly reduced medical costs arising from early identification and treatment of individual mental health and substance use issues."[60]

Not all companies and organizations offer EAP services. Also, the services available through EAP programs vary from organization to organization. It's your responsibility to know whether or not your organization offers an EAP program. If your organization does offer EAP services, find out how you can refer employees to the program, what services the program provides, and how you can use the program to support employees' success in the workplace. Perhaps your organization has a brochure or webpage you can share with employees. Keep these resources at your fingertips. Remember to work with your direct manager or human resources when assisting employees with any sensitive issues.

The Impact of Addictions in the Workplace

I interviewed Scott H. Silverman, CEO of Confidential Recovery, an outpatient program in San Diego, California, allowing clients to continue their careers or jobs and enjoy living at home while receiving long-term therapy.[61] Scott is the recipient of numerous honors and awards and an expert in workforce development. He's also an acclaimed speaker and the author of *Tell Me No, I Dare You: A Guide for Living a Heroic Life*.

Thirty years ago he was struggling with addiction and, after a failed suicide attempt, he left home and immediately entered treatment. Today, he's a living testimony to transformation and healing. He's now 31 years sober and working to empower others on their journey.

Scott shared that "15% of the population has a potential active addiction and, over the next 12 months," their addiction will negatively impact "7 to 10 people they run into throughout the day, whether it's someone on the road driving or someone's family... That's almost 85% of the population." Scott underscored how people with addictions affect their family, their community, and the workforce. He said that individuals with addictions negatively impact productivity and noted that "it's a very interesting phenomenon that isn't looked at by leadership... Leadership is more focused on the person, and it's hard to measure how it impacts others."[62]

Based on the detrimental impact addictions have on society and the workplace, it behooves organizations to identify when individuals have addictions and to provide them the support they need.

Identifying Addictions in the Workplace

Scott pointed out that managers and supervisors can keep an eye out for signs that may indicate an addiction, be it drugs, alcohol, gambling, or something else. He said these signs could be "anything as simple as attendance, behavior, attitude change, all those things that impact the bottom line... When someone's behavior starts to shift, it's clear. You know someone's coming in late or having extended lunches that are not scheduled. They smell of alcohol. They go to sleep at their desk. They're disoriented. There's all kinds of weight loss, weight gains, or other 'tells' if you look closely. And sometimes you don't have to look too closely. They're obvious."[63]

Once managers and supervisors have identified that a person may potentially have an addiction, Scott recommends that they discreetly ask questions in a manner that isn't offensive or intrusive. He said that it's best to ask, "Is everything okay? Is there anything I can do?" He also emphasized that it would be inappropriate to ask a direct question, such as, "By the way, I noticed that your productivity is off by 22% and we think you might have a drinking problem." Scott reminded us that "sometimes you need to bring in the experts."[64]

This is where company EAP programs can play a role, but encouraging employees to take advantage of this resource is sometimes challenging.

Employees Are Leery about EAPs

In my experience, employees are hesitant to take advantage of EAP services, even when informed that the program is confidential.

Scott explained that employees are afraid of the stigma, of being branded or pigeonholed and losing opportunities as a result. He told the story of a person who was reluctant to disclose mental health issues for fear it would cost him his job. The mental health issues escalated to such a degree that the person committed suicide. Reflecting on this tragic loss of life, Scott noted, "We just have to create a work environment where, whatever is going on with our team, we let them know that there is somebody there, and if there isn't somebody there, that there's a number. There's a resource they can call to ask questions in a safe, confidential environment... We need to make it easier for people to get help earlier versus later."[65]

The Bottom Line of Well-Being

I asked Scott how leaders can balance support and accountability in these sensitive situations. Demonstrating his servant's heart, he answered, "We're always talking about the bottom line. We're always talking about performance measures, outcomes. I think part of what we also need to talk about is well-being... Are you happy at work? Is there something we can do to add value to your environment?"[66] Scott's wisdom is a testament to how simply caring about the people you lead and serve will positively impact the workplace and the bottom line.

You can get more information about Scott H. Silverman and his company, Confidential Recovery, at www.confidentialrecovery.com.

The Family and Medical Leave Act

Another resource available to employees facing personal and family medical conditions is The Family and Medical Leave Act (FMLA). The U.S. Department of Labor, Wage and Hour Division defines FMLA as follows:

"The Family and Medical Leave Act (FMLA) provides certain employees with up to 12 weeks of unpaid, job-protected leave per year. It also requires that their group health benefits be maintained during the leave. FMLA is designed to help employees balance their work and family responsibilities by allowing them to take reasonable unpaid leave for certain family and medical reasons. It also seeks to accommodate the legitimate interests of employers and promote equal employment opportunity for men and women. FMLA applies to all public agencies, all public and private elementary and secondary schools, and companies with 50 or more employees."[67]

You can read about the federal laws, regulations, and guidance governing FMLA by visiting the Department of Labor's FMLA website at https://www.dol.gov/general/topic/benefits-leave/fmla. However, please note that each state and organization has specific policies, procedures, and paperwork for the administration of FMLA.[68] Your manager or your designated human resources professional can share information about your organization's FMLA policies and procedures.

If you have an employee who is struggling to meet attendance expectations, you may need to determine if FMLA is warranted or if you need to take another course of action. Seek guidance from your manager and human resources experts.

Workers' Compensation

When an employee suffers a work-related injury, illness, or exposure, refer the employee to the workers' compensation program if appropriate. Again, seek guidance from your manager and HR. According to Ann Clayton, *"Workers' compensation programs in the United States are state regulated, with laws determined by each state legislative body and implemented by a state agency. The programs provide the payment of lost wages, medical treatment, and rehabilitation services to workers suffering from an occupational injury or disease."*[69]

In some states, certain companies and organizations are not required to provide workers' compensation programs to their employees.[70] Find out from your manager or human resources department what your organization's policies and procedures are for workers' compensation before an employee work-related injury or illness arises. If your organization offers workers' compensation, have all policies, procedures, forms, and contact information handy.

Americans with Disabilities Act

Employees can also have a disability that can affect their ability to function in general or to meet performance and behavior expectations. If an employee discloses or you suspect a disability, it's imperative that you immediately notify your manager and human resources to ensure compliance with the Americans with Disabilities Act (ADA).

The United States Department of Justice and Civil Rights Division provides the following overview regarding ADA:

"The ADA is one of America's most comprehensive pieces of civil rights legislation that prohibits discrimination and guarantees that people with disabilities have the same opportunities as everyone else to participate in the mainstream of American life—to enjoy employment opportunities, to purchase goods and services, and to participate in State and local government programs and services... To be

protected by the ADA, one must have a disability, which is defined by the ADA as a physical or mental impairment that substantially limits one or more major life activities, a person who has a history or record of such an impairment, or a person who is perceived by others as having such an impairment. The ADA doesn't specifically name all of the impairments that are covered."[71]

Your manager or human resources expert can guide you in cases involving FMLA, ADA, workers' compensation, or other sensitive situations. Due to the legal implications, it's critical that you don't attempt to navigate these types of situations without adequate guidance from your organization's designated parties. Depending on the size and structure of your organization, these may include human resources, labor relations, risk management, legal counsel, and the like. It's vital that you know your organization's protocol.

> *Documentation Tip: When employees experience hardships, their performance, mindset, and behavior may be impacted. Seek the guidance of your manager, human resources experts, legal counsel, or other experts from your organization on how to provide support and appropriately document the facts.*

In Review

To drive performance, you must identify and meet the support needs of employees. These needs will vary by industry, occupation, and individual. While it's impractical to create an exhaustive list of these needs, some critical support factors are common in the workplace. These include tools, equipment, supplies, training, and access to information. Other support factors may include EAP programs, FMLA, workers' compensation, and ADA workplace accommodations. These are only some of the possible support needs for employee success. Support needs are unique to the individual. The more you get to know each employee by establishing and maintaining a strong supervisor-employee relationship, the better you will be able to identify and satisfy each employee's needs.

Putting It into Action

1. Gather information about the resources available to employees through your organization and keep this information accessible.

2. During your recurring individual conferences, ask employees what support they need to be successful.

3. If an employee is struggling with attendance, punctuality, performance or behavior, identify the person's support needs and develop a plan to meet these needs. Share this information with your manager and human resources following your organization's protocol.

Chapter 9
The Power of Employee Recognition

In a culture of appreciation, employee recognition isn't limited to a top-down approach, but rather reaches far and wide into the organization.

Employee recognition is a powerful tool for engaging employees, promoting great organizational performance,[72] and achieving customer service excellence.[73] It's a vital element that influences employee motivation,[74] satisfaction, and commitment to the organization.[75] Recognition lets employees know their contributions towards the goals of the organization are acknowledged and appreciated.[76]

SUPPORTIVE ACCOUNTABILITY LEADERSHIP™

Defining Employee Recognition

The leadership and management literature provides various definitions for employee recognition. In the Supportive Accountability Leadership Model, the definition of *employee recognition* is "showing employees they're appreciated and shining a light on great performance." This simple definition goes much deeper than formalized employee recognition programs. It focuses on creating a culture of appreciation. In this type of environment, a sincere expression of gratitude qualifies as recognition.

In a culture of appreciation, employee recognition isn't limited to a top-down approach, but rather reaches far and wide into the organization. It can be peer-to-peer, supervisor-to-employee, employee-to-supervisor, and many other combinations. This requires you to actively recognize employees, and more importantly, to build a culture where everyone in the workplace is inspired to appreciate one another.

Recognition Promotes a Great Workplace

When leaders create a culture where employees feel valued, appreciated and supported, they have a positive impact on overall employee satisfaction and mental health. Recognition empowers and mentally strengthens employees, giving them resilience against the demands of the job and the associated pressures. Being valued at work and being emotionally supported by one's leaders is associated with lower levels of burnout and stress.[77] When you continuously build employees' resilience through recognition and positive feedback, you create an emotionally supportive environment that gives them the strength and motivation to handle the challenges that come along the way.

Employee recognition also promotes satisfied and motivated employees who are inspired to serve and satisfy customers.[78] And satisfied customers have a direct, positive impact on your organization's bottom line. Recognition also reinforces the organization's expectations, priorities, and values. This reinforcement focuses employees' time, energy, and talent on what matters most, which promotes strong employee performance and advances the organization's vision.

Employee Recognition Isn't Optional

Everyone needs to be recognized. Employee recognition is an integral part of employee feedback and rewards. Through recognition, you're affirming to employees that they're either meeting or exceeding expectations and that their achievements are appreciated. Recognition tells employees they're on the right track, which develops and strengthens their self-confidence. By giving employees continuous positive feedback, you're not making them guess how they're performing.

Recognition isn't just for star employees who stand out in the crowd, but also for those who do their work quietly behind the scenes and even for those who are struggling but making a sincere effort to improve. Don't be afraid to recognize employees for exceptional performance in one area, even if they're struggling in another. Their performance difficulties in one area shouldn't cast a negative shadow on what they're doing well. Similarly, when employees are facing roadblocks, celebrate each step forward the employee takes on the road to success. Demonstrating appreciation for struggling employees when they do well builds their self-confidence, encourages them to exert more effort to improve, and helps them view constructive feedback as support rather than criticism.

The Elements of Effective Employee Recognition

For recognition and praise to be effective, you can't let it go on autopilot. You need to be intentional. To make employee recognition powerful, deliver it immediately, make it valuable to the employee, and provide it for real accomplishments.[79]

Timely, Specific, and Meaningful

Be timely and specific in your recognition and do it for something meaningful. As soon as you observe great performance, give recognition and praise. Point out the particular action and why it's worthy of praise. Avoid relying on easy phrases like "great job" and "good work." While there's nothing wrong with including these types of phrases in your recognition, they alone don't sound either sincere or meaningful. For recognition to have an impact, add the specifics. For example, you may write: "Jane, I appreciate you dropping everything to help us meet the grant application deadline! I know it was a last-minute request, yet you jumped right in with a cheerful attitude. Thank you for your service to families in need!" This will take more time and thought. However, it will let Jane know that her sacrifice and contributions were noticed and appreciated. It will also reinforce the organization's greater good.

Frequent

Recognition and positive feedback must be frequent.[80] It's not sufficient to recognize employees at the annual employee recognition event. Even once a month isn't enough. In a culture of appreciation, recognition happens on a daily basis, because people are genuinely grateful. If this sounds excessive, remember that recognition can take many shapes, doesn't have to be formal, and can be provided by everyone in the organization. Focus your energy on creating a culture of appreciation, and you won't be the only person recognizing employees; you will inspire people to express their gratitude to one another freely. This significantly increases the opportunities for employees to receive recognition in the workplace. However, you must still keep an eye out for stellar performance, both quantitative and qualitative, and recognize it.

Varied

Recognition doesn't have to be costly. It can take on a variety of forms, and it can happen at the individual or group level.

Individualized

People are unique, and not everyone likes to be recognized in the same way. Get to know employees individually and ask them how they like to be recognized. Some employees love being in the spotlight of a big employee recognition event, while others would be horrified at the public display. Some employees prefer money. Others enjoy some time off. Find out how each employee wants to be recognized. Failure to honor their preferences can backfire and result in recognition that demotivates them.

Recognition Gone Wrong

Shelly was a quiet and productive YouthZone employee who was under Vic's supervision. In fact, she was consistently the top producer of the entire Youth Employment Program. She enjoyed close relationships with people who were important to her, but she was private and didn't share openly with most of her co-workers. She also didn't like a lot of attention.

Less than two years ago, when Vic was a new supervisor, he decided to recognize Shelly because of her consistent outstanding job placement and job retention statistics throughout the calendar year.

So he nominated her for a coveted award. Vic's former manager, Tim, selected Shelly for the prize.

At Tim's direction, the Award Committee planned for weeks to surprise Shelly at the annual staff meeting, which consisted of 150 YouthZone employees from all departments and programs in the organization.

On the day of the event, Tim called Shelly to the stage, which was front and center of a large auditorium. Shelly timidly made her approach, the lights shining brightly on her. With great enthusiasm, Tim touted how fantastic Shelly's performance had been that year. He even provided hard data to prove it. Tim concluded his lively speech by presenting Shelly with an engraved plaque and monetary award, as everyone gave her an enthusiastic standing ovation. During the entire presentation, Shelly stood stiffly on the stage, rubbing her hands and staring at the floor. But Tim was too excited to notice.

In the weeks that followed, Shelly's performance dipped. She was still meeting YouthZone's performance goals but was no longer delivering stellar results. Tim and Vic didn't understand that the recognition they had viewed as a special reward for Shelly, she saw differently. She was so embarrassed by the public spectacle that she decided she would never do anything that would get her this type of attention again. Unfortunately, Vic had not taken the time to get to know Shelly before nominating her for the award.

Ways to Recognize

Here are some ways you can recognize employees:

Words of Appreciation

Use your words to show employees you appreciate them and what they do. Do this frequently, so they know their contributions are not taken for granted. A simple "thank you," when done in a meaningful and sincere manner, goes a long way.

The Creative "Thank You" Email

Send an email of appreciation. Take a few extra minutes to choose the right words to make the email meaningful. Add clip art or a beautiful picture that conveys the spirit of your message and change the color and font of the letters to tie it all together. This takes more time than sending a generic message. However, it communicates that the accomplishment was worthy enough for you to give it some thought.

Inspirational Cards

Purchase cards with inspirational quotes or pictures, or a stack of "thank you" notes, and keep them at your desk. When you catch an employee in the act of doing something great, take out a card and write a short, handwritten note of appreciation for that person. A handwritten note gives your expression of appreciation a personal touch.

Wendi Pomerance Brick, President and CEO of Customer Service Advantage, Inc., emphasized how valuable a simple "thank you" card can be. She shared her experience giving cards to employees who did exceptionally well in her mystery shopping programs. Wendi said, "After people were mystery shopped, I gave a handwritten note to everyone who scored all fives. I wrote something like, 'You were shopped on this date, this time, and you got a perfect rating. Thank you so much for going out of your way to provide great service to our customers!' I would write something to them and it was one of my favorite things to do. I would take home a stack of cards, and write them in the evening. I loved it, because I was able to see all this wonderful work and acknowledge people were doing a great job. Periodically, I even had people show me that they kept their cards!"[81]

Wendi recognized employees for their great customer service, even if they had performance issues in other areas. She explained, "Even if there is something else going on, in this moment, on this date, at this time, they did a great job. And that's what I cared about."[82]

Special Roles, Projects, and Tasks

One frequently overlooked form of recognition is the assignment of special roles, projects, and tasks. Selecting employees for one of these choice assignments tells them you trust them, acknowledge their talent, and believe in their capabilities. It not only recognizes employees, but it develops their potential.

A Star Is Born

Vic was on a two-week vacation, and his backup supervisor was covering his unit. Vic's right arm, a strong lead counselor named Rebecca, was providing most of the day-to-day support to the team in Vic's absence. The backup supervisor was available to guide Rebecca as needed and to handle sensitive administrative tasks that were not appropriate for Rebecca to address. However, Rebecca was a seasoned employee and knew exactly what to do to keep things running smoothly.

While Vic was out, Alex received a call from a company requesting a presentation from the Youth Employment Program. The company's HR department wanted to know how the program could help them hire local youth for paid summer internships. The supervisor covering the unit was highly knowledgeable in the program but didn't particularly enjoy presentations. Therefore, Alex decided to ask Rebecca to present. Rebecca had delivered presentations before with excellent outcomes.

Alex called Rebecca to her office and discussed the company's request. She explained the importance of the presentation and asked Rebecca to deliver it given her knowledge, excellent presentation skills, and professionalism. Rebecca gave Alex a big smile and said she would be happy to help.

When Rebecca walked out of the office, Alex's secretary immediately popped in. "Alex, what did you say to Rebecca? You should have seen her face. She looked so happy. I would've thought she just got a big promotion!"

What seemed like just a simple assignment to Alex was, in fact, a significant form of recognition for Rebecca.

Employee-of-the-Month Program

Institute an employee-of-the-month program and select one recipient each month. You can sweeten the pot by offering the recipient a reserved parking spot if employees don't typically have one. You can also add a certificate, a trophy, or a combination of other tangible prizes. Post an employee-of-the-month plaque in a prominent location, where you can display the names and pictures of the award recipients on a monthly basis. In addition to recognizing employees, a prominently displayed employee-of-the-month award promotes a positive atmosphere.

Certificates

Issue certificates of appreciation and recognition. Don't print them on regular copy paper. Keep certificate paper, seals, ribbons, and folders on hand. You can purchase these at any office supply store.

You can also opt to use templates from word processing software. However, the look and feel of nice certificate paper can increase the employee's perception of value. Invest in the necessary supplies to make the recognition memorable.

Recognition Plaques and Trophies

Purchase employee recognition plaques and trophies. They come in various shapes and sizes, from the simple to the elaborate. They can also become prized possessions, especially when they have the employee's name and a customized message engraved on them.

Branded Giveaways

Give away promotional items with your organization's logo and an inspirational message. They come in the form of pens, coffee mugs, letter openers, stress balls, lanyards, lunch boxes, totes, and much more. In addition to expressing your appreciation, these giveaways promote your organization's brand and strengthen employees' identity as valued members of your organization.

Gift Cards

If you know employees well, you can give them a gift card to their favorite store or venue. This could be a coffee shop, tea shop, gardening store, sporting goods store, movie theater, or another vendor. You can place the gift card inside an inspirational card, make it part of a themed gift basket, or combine it with a formal certificate or letter.

Monetary and Time-Off Awards

Issue a certificate or letter signed by your president, director, or another executive along with a cash or time-off award. A signature from upper management adds value to the award.

Monetary Bonuses

Provide performance-based cash bonuses. Make sure employees know they were awarded based on performance.

> *Documentation Tip: File copies of recognition issued to employees in their files. This documentation will be useful when you write their performance evaluations.*

Themed Wall of Appreciation

Dedicate an entire wall for employees to thank one another. They can do so peer-to-peer, supervisor-to-employee, and employee-to-supervisor. This wall can spark the fire of gratitude in your office. To encourage employee participation, keep it simple. Avoid bureaucratic requirements, screening processes, and other cumbersome procedures. If the process for using the themed wall is complicated or leadership approval is required, it will discourage employee participation.

Involve employees in coming up with a theme and decorating the wall. Invite them to develop a simple process for using the wall and announce it to other employees. On a regular basis, select some of the notes of appreciation and share them in newsletters, at staff meetings, in public- and employee-facing electronic message boards, and other fun avenues. As you get employees excited about appreciating others, you will start to see a shift towards a culture of appreciation.

Electronic Message Board

Use electronic message boards to display exciting and fresh information with your staff and customers every day. Include inspirational quotes and messages of appreciation for the team and individuals. Share updates on fun activities, events, projects, and initiatives. Celebrate victories large and small, from notable performance outcomes to small steps in the right direction. Show pictures of employees in action, working hard and playing hard. Incorporate graphs, charts, and creative fonts and colors that grab attention and make the electronic message board fun and exciting.

Recognition Meal

Recognize employees with a tasty and healthy meal. Food provides sustenance. When you break bread with employees, you're doing more than recognizing them. You're sharing time, speaking with them, and establishing a stronger connection. You're saying, "I value spending time with you." You can either take employees out to eat or bring food to the office, as long as the environment is suitable and free of distractions.

Employee Recognition Event

Host an employee recognition event for your entire unit, office, or division. Engage employees in the planning process. The affair can be as simple as an office cookout or as elaborate as a catered off-site event. Get creative.

In Review

Effective employee recognition is much broader than a formalized program and creates a culture of appreciation. Research demonstrates that recognition has a positive impact on employees' physical and mental health, satisfaction, commitment, and overall well-being. It also influences organizational performance and customer satisfaction. Because of these benefits, employee recognition isn't optional. As a leader, you're responsible for ensuring that employees are being recognized and appreciated for their contributions in the workplace.

Putting It into Action

1. Privately ask employees how they would like to be recognized for exceptional performance. Make a note in their employee file, so that you can refer to it.

2. Buy inspirational cards to use for on-the-spot appreciation.

3. Develop an employee recognition plan and include various ways to recognize employees.

4. Involve employees in developing a wall of appreciation. Ask them to select a theme, develop simple procedures, and spread the word.

Chapter 10
The 4 P's of Accountability™

Accountability isn't about using the stick to beat employees
into meeting performance expectations… Holding employees
accountable is the caring thing to do.

Accountability isn't a four-letter word. It's not something bad you do to people. Holding employees accountable is the caring thing to do. When you hold yourself and employees accountable, you're reinforcing expectations, ensuring they have all the tools they need to be successful, and cheering for them when they succeed.

SUPPORTIVE ACCOUNTABILITY LEADERSHIP™

Accountability isn't about using the stick to beat employees into meeting performance expectations. Taking this approach only leads to unsupportive accountability. This may achieve the intended performance results, but at a significant cost to the employee, to you, to the organization, and ultimately to your customers. Likewise, operating with a complete lack of accountability creates a reactive work environment, where you're dealing with the excessive unplanned shifting of work and unnecessary traffic from upset customers, be it in person, via telephone, or electronic.

It's more efficient to hold employees accountable and work in a proactive environment than to face unnecessary chaos. Holding employees accountable takes time, energy, and resources. However, letting issues snowball out of control will require a lot more work on your part. It may require the intervention of others, which doesn't make you look good as a leader. It can also cause you stress, anxiety, sleepless nights, your reputation, and even your job. Instead, supportive accountability aims at understanding employees' support needs and helping them achieve success.

The 4 P's of Accountability™

As a leader, an essential part of your job is to get work done through others. You're responsible for holding yourself and employees accountable for meeting performance goals and objectives. The 4 P's of Accountability is the accountability framework I developed as part of the Supportive Accountability Leadership Model. This framework consists of four principles—people, purpose, performance, and progression.

People

People matter. Period.

People are your organization's most important resource. People drive performance[83]—not technology, performance goals, strategy, or anything else. As you promote accountability, help people feel safe, valued, and cared about.

Leading with Supportive Accountability

Supportive accountability can help you work effectively with people. It's the most balanced and effective of the four leadership styles in the Supportive Accountability Leadership Model.

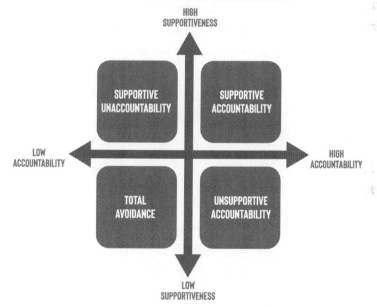

FOUR LEADERSHIP STYLES OF SUPPORTIVE ACCOUNTABILITY™

Leaders who manage performance with supportive accountability hold themselves and employees jointly accountable for successful performance. They also provide employees with the support critical to their success. Getting to know employees on a personal level and establishing a strong supervisor-employee relationship will help you uncover these support needs.

People Need Fairness

People need to feel they're being treated fairly in the workplace, especially when it comes to accountability. Employees observe and assess manager and supervisor interactions with each other and with other employees. They also compare stories about how fairly managers and supervisors treated them. Whether these accounts are accurate or not, they influence how employees collectively view the fairness of their leadership and their organization.[84]

Employees React Negatively to Unfairness

Employees react negatively when they feel managers or supervisors are unfair to their co-workers, regardless of whether or not they're friends with them.[85] However, when employees feel they're the targets of unfairness, the adverse reaction is stronger.[86] How you manage employees' reactions will serve to either dispel their perceptions of injustice or reinforce them. Don't take employees' reactions personally; respond with caring and compassion.

Unfairness Destroys Employee Motivation

Employee perception of fairness in the workplace is one of the top elements influencing employee satisfaction. A workplace environment perceived by employees as fair promotes employee satisfaction and increases morale, whereas a workplace viewed as unfair has a detrimental effect on employee motivation and well-being.[87] When unfairness permeates the environment, employees are not motivated to bring their best to work.

Unfairness Makes Employees Sick

The level of workplace fairness affects the emotional, psychological, and physical well-being of employees. Vigorous longitudinal studies have linked supervisor unfairness to "medically certified sickness absences (Kivimaki et al., 2003), coronary heart disease (Kivimaki et al., 2005), and cardiovascular deaths (Eloviano et al., 2006)."[88]

Unfairness Hurts Your Organization

Employee illness, burnout, and workplace stress take a significant toll on organizational performance. When employees frequently call out sick or report to work in poor physical and emotional shape, productivity suffers. There's also a negative impact on workplace interpersonal relationships, customer satisfaction, and quality of work. Burned-out, stressed-out, and sick employees are not able to bring their best to work even if they want to. Consequently, an unfair and unhealthy work environment will suffer a significant loss of talent, as employees explore their options and find better places to work.

You Play a Crucial Role

As a manager or supervisor, you play a crucial role in shaping employee attitudes about their workplace, and this includes employee perceptions about fairness. Research demonstrates that the direct supervisor impacts employees' opinions about workplace fairness much more than the organization itself.[89] Unfairness during supervisor-employee interactions has a more significant impact on employee burnout and workplace stress than that related to the distribution of outcomes, rights, and resources.[90] These findings accentuate the remarkable influence that you wield in shaping the perception of fairness in the workplace. For your organization to have a vibrant and productive workforce, developing your leadership skills to promote objectivity during the accountability process is a priority.

Purpose

The goal of accountability isn't to punish, but rather to create a supportive work environment where employees can thrive and drive performance. In this vein, the purpose of accountability is to advance your organization's vision, focus on achieving its goals, empower employees to perform, and account for progress and results.

Advancing the Vision

Accountability advances your organization's vision and mission. Continuously articulate the vision and how the work they collectively do makes a difference. This helps employees see the purpose of their work, rather than merely focusing on a laundry list of duties and tasks.

Focusing on What Matters

Accountability helps you and employees get clear about the team's goals and how these goals advance the organization's greater good. Often our work environment has so many goals and objectives that they become overwhelming. Accountability helps us prioritize our goals, develop a strategy to achieve them, and zero in on what matters most.

Empowering Employees to Perform

In supportive accountability, your role is to set employees up for success and empowering them to take ownership. The rest is up to them.

Accounting for Progress and Results

A healthy supervisor-employee relationship requires both the supervisor and the employee to account for progress and results. As a leader, you provide an update regarding the status of the critical resources the employee needs to succeed. Likewise, employees explain their progress in achieving performance goals. This requires honesty, transparency, and mutual support.

Performance

Accountability focuses on performance and ensures everyone is contributing to the organization's success.

Focusing on Performance Boosts Morale

The work that underperforming employees leave behind, either through absences, tardiness, lack of productivity, or incompetence, has to be completed by someone else. Likewise, the disgruntled customer who didn't get her needs met by an underperforming employee will need to be served by someone. That someone is most likely a high-performing employee, who completes the work of others as his "reward." If you consistently shift the unfinished or substandard work of underperforming employees without holding them accountable, you will create a disengaging environment for those who work hard. Also, your best employees will start looking for a better place to work.

Addressing performance issues is the caring thing to do for employees who are achieving results and for those who are experiencing difficulty and need your support to improve.

Don't Compromise

As you focus on performance, don't compromise your integrity or ethics. It's equally important to avoid the appearance of compromise. It's far better to report poor performance and have the satisfaction of improving it the right way than to lose your reputation, your sleep, your job, or even your freedom because of inappropriate activities. Also, remember that people matter. Don't sacrifice the health, safety, and well-being of people for the sake of performance.

Progression

Accountability requires progression, the act of moving forward through continuous improvement until performance goals are achieved. When employees are doing well, it involves catapulting performance to higher levels. When employees are struggling, progression is the act of moving forward to help employees meet expectations.

The Performance Improvement Plan

The Performance Improvement Plan (PIP) is a tool you can use during progression. It's a written plan that lays out the steps necessary for an employee to improve his or her performance. It describes the support and accountability the employee needs to succeed. It also documents the support you have already provided. How and when you use the PIP for performance improvement depends on your organization's HR policies, approach, and philosophy.

The Basic Elements of a PIP. The format of a PIP varies from organization to organization. However, it usually contains some basic elements.

- **PIP Start and End Dates:** The duration of a PIP can vary, depending on the specific circumstances. I have used PIPs in increments of 30, 60, and 90 days, depending on a variety of factors.

- **Performance Areas that Need Improvement:** Note the broader performance areas where the employee hasn't met expectations.

- **Performance Expectations/Standards:** State the performance expectations and standards the employee hasn't met. If these expectations are in writing, cite source documents.

- **Examples of the Substandard Performance:** Provide specific examples of performance that hasn't met the expectations and standards that have been communicated. List dates when performance issues occurred, as well as any coaching, feedback, and support provided.

- **PIP Goals:** Identify specific goals to be achieved during the PIP to meet expectations and standards. Ensure these goals are measurable so you can quantify progress. These goals must align with the performance expectations and standards that need improvement.

- **Monitoring:** Explain the method and frequency you will use to measure employee progress in meeting the PIP goals.

- **Feedback:** Indicate how often you and the employee will meet to discuss the employee's progress in achieving the PIP goals. Establish the meeting schedule. I prefer weekly meetings because it helps the employee maintain focus, receive support, and achieve success.

- **Support:** Identify the specific support you will provide the employee to help her succeed.

- **Consequences for Not Meeting the PIP Goals:** Clarify what the consequences will be if the employee doesn't meet the stated goals by the end of the PIP.

PIP language and formats vary widely from organization to organization. Seek guidance from your manager or human resources as you implement the PIP. They may, in turn, consult with legal counsel, labor relations, risk management, or other appropriate departments to mitigate risk.

Vic Implements a PIP

Mary had completed the two-hour online training, and Vic had encouraged her to apply what she had learned. Vic had already met with Mary several times and emphasized that her customer service challenges couldn't continue. He had even issued her written documentation of their last two conversations. But things didn't improve.

Since then, Mary had received several negative customer satisfaction surveys. After each one of them, Vic had consulted with Alex and HR and had provided Mary immediate feedback. He had also documented everything, just like he had been advised to do. He had spent numerous hours on this issue alone, but Mary's customer service still wasn't improving.

After consulting with Alex and the HR manager yet one more time, Vic implemented a 30-Day PIP to help Mary succeed. This 30-day period was the timeframe the HR manager had previously used with another supervisor for an employee who had struggled with similar customer service issues. The HR manager emphasized that Vic would be expected to provide extensive support to ensure Mary had the best opportunity to succeed. Vic knew this would require significant time and energy, but he desperately needed this nightmare to end. It had gone on long enough.

The HR manager and Alex approved the following PIP:

- **PIP Start and End Dates:** August 7th to September 7th

- **Performance Areas that Need Improvement:** Customer service

- **Performance Expectations/Standards:**

  Per YouthZone's Youth Employment Customer Service Expectations:

  - **Customer Satisfaction:** Achieve an average customer satisfaction rating or 4 or higher in all customer satisfaction areas measured.

156

- **Customer Complaint Prevention:** Receive zero valid customer complaints.

- **Examples of the Substandard Performance:** Vic listed examples of how Mary had not met the expectations. These included specific dates and incidents, and the data on Mary's Customer Satisfaction Reports.

- **PIP Goals:** On a weekly basis, meet the following customer service standards:

  - **Customer Complaint Prevention:** Receive zero valid customer complaints.

  - **Customer Satisfaction:** Achieve an average customer satisfaction rating or 4 or higher in all customer satisfaction areas measured.

- **Monitoring:** On a weekly basis, Vic would:

  - Print a copy of Mary's Monthly Customer Satisfaction Report for the week

  - Use a survey tool to conduct five random customer satisfaction telephone surveys of customers Mary served during the week

  - Keep a log of any verbal customer compliments and complaints for the week

- **Feedback:** Vic and Mary would meet each Friday at 3:00 p.m. in the huddle room to discuss her progress and support needs.

- **Support:** Vic would provide the following support:

  - Two-hour, one-time customer service training during the first week of the PIP

  - Weekly one-hour online training during the remaining three weeks of the PIP

- Workload reduction to allow Mary sufficient to participate in training

- Provide Mary a journal where she can take notes during training, self-reflect, and record how she applied what she learned in her customer interactions

- **Consequences for Not Meeting Standards:** If Mary doesn't meet the customer service standards by the end of the PIP, it may result in disciplinary action.

In Review

The 4 P's of Accountability consist of the following principles that hold supervisors and employees accountable for achieving strong performance:

1. People – People matter; balance accountability with support.

2. Purpose – The purpose of accountability is to create a supportive work environment where people can thrive and drive performance.

3. Performance – Focus on performance.

4. Progression – Progress until you attain the desired outcome.

These principles will help you achieve supportive accountability to boost performance.

Putting It into Action

1. People – Increase employees' perception of fairness in the accountability process. When performance isn't up to par, help the employee feel safe, valued, and cared about. Talk to the employee and ask her what she needs to be successful.

2. Purpose – Prominently display and emphasize your

organization's mission and vision, leveraging any branded materials created by your organization. Continuously clarify goals, objectives, and expectations.

3. Performance – When employees are underperforming, don't shift their work to others. Hold them accountable.

4. Progression – If you find yourself stuck in a never-ending cycle of clarifying expectations, monitoring performance, facilitating feedback conversations, and providing support without seeing improvement, it's time to progress. The problem won't correct itself, and you will soon find yourself feeling frustrated. Seek guidance from your manager and human resources to apply progressive discipline.

Chapter 11
Boosting Performance through Progressive Discipline

Implement progressive discipline in the spirit of support.

Progressive discipline is a tool to help employees improve performance and behavior through progressive levels of supportive teaching and correction. Implement progressive discipline in the spirit of support.

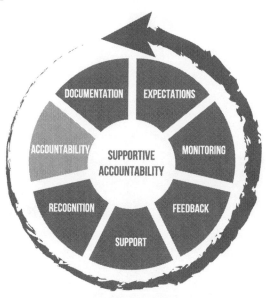

SUPPORTIVE ACCOUNTABILITY LEADERSHIP™

The purpose of progressive discipline is to help employees improve performance. However, employees often find the process uncomfortable, as receiving feedback isn't easy when one isn't meeting expectations.

Your goal is to leverage the progressive discipline process to improve performance while promoting a great work environment where employees are happy, perform better, and are committed to the success of your organization. To accomplish this goal, coach employees as soon as performance or behavioral difficulties arise. This will give them the opportunity to correct problems at the lowest possible level. However, when performance doesn't improve, it does require that you assess the need for progression through the various levels of discipline.

The Final Results of Mary's PIP

It was the second week of September, and Mary's PIP had ended the previous week. Vic had already met with her to review the results of the final week of the PIP. Today, after consulting with Alex and the HR manager, Vic was meeting with Mary to discuss the final results of the entire 30-day period.

Here is what Vic shared with Mary:

Week	Meeting Date	Standard Met?: Zero Valid Complaints	Standard Met?: Average Customer Satisfaction Ratings of 4 or Higher in All Areas Measured
1	August 11th	N	N
2	August 18th	Y	N
3	August 25th	Y	Y
4	September 1st	Y	Y
5	September 7th	Y	Y
SUMMARY:		Standard met 80% (4 of 5) of weeks on PIP	Standard met 60% (3 of 5) weeks on PIP

During the five weeks of Mary's PIP, she met the standard of receiving zero valid customer complaints 80% of the time. She met the standard of achieving average customer satisfaction ratings of 4 or higher in all areas rated 60% of the time. While Mary didn't achieve 100% of the two goals, the results showed that she was making an effort to improve. She received complaints during her first week on the PIP but not in the weeks that followed. Also, while she didn't meet the customer satisfaction requirements during her first two weeks on the PIP, she met them in the last three weeks. Mary was sincerely trying to improve. At the direction of Alex and the HR manager, Vic let Mary know that the PIP would be extended for another 30 days to give her more time to meet the standards.

At the end of the second 30-day period, Mary met the expectation in every week of the PIP and averted discipline. Not only did the complaints stop coming in, but Vic received some odd but welcome compliments about Mary during his telephone surveys. One youth said, "I used to be afraid to call Mary because she was always rude. But this last time, she was a different person." Another youth said, "Mary was so nice and helpful the last time I called her. I thought it was weird. But I'm happy about it." Vic shared these comments with Mary to show her that her customers were noticing the improvement.

The PIP had been time-consuming for Vic, but the results were completely worth it. He had invested a significant amount of time clarifying expectations, monitoring progress, and providing feedback and support. But now Mary was on the right track. Alex was no longer calling Vic into her office to address complaints. He could now dedicate more time to what he loved to do—leading his team into being the best.

The story of Mary ended well. Alex and Vic achieved the primary goal of supportive accountability: to provide the support and accountability to help Mary succeed. However, it could have ended differently.

Two Alternative Endings

There were two other possible endings. In the first, Mary could have discovered through the process that the youth employment specialist position wasn't a good fit for her and voluntarily moved on to another role. Whether this role was one at YouthZone or outside the organization, it would have been a "win-win-win" for Vic, Mary, and YouthZone. In the second possible outcome, Mary would have continued to underperform in spite of the extensive support provided, and Vic would have gone down the discipline path with the guidance of Alex and the human resources manager. Discipline was never the goal, but it would have been necessary to support customers, other employees, and the organization.

Five Levels of Progressive Discipline

The levels of progressive discipline vary from organization to organization. However, these are five frequently used levels:

1. Verbal Warning

2. Written Warning

3. Suspension

4. Demotion

5. Termination

Some organizations have fewer levels than those listed above. Some have more. Some have different names for their levels. However, they're all part of the progressive discipline process. Your organization has specific language, rules, policies, procedures, and protocols regarding progressive discipline. Take the time to learn how your organization administers this process. Ask your manager or human resources experts to point you to official policies, training, and job aids that can help you understand the levels of discipline for your organization. This knowledge will prove highly beneficial throughout your leadership career with your organization.

The Progressive Nature of Discipline

Regardless of the levels of discipline your organization uses, the process is usually progressive. Your goal is for the employee to improve performance or behavior without the need for discipline. However, if the employee doesn't improve at lower levels, you may need to progress as appropriate.

In spite of the name, you won't always progress through the levels of discipline. Sometimes it's necessary to either repeat a level or apply a lower level than the last. This may be the case when either a new type of issue has surfaced or too much time has lapsed between similar occurrences. On the other hand, if the incident is severe, as in the case of theft, workplace violence, or intoxication on the job, the lower levels may be skipped altogether, and the incident may lead to termination. This will depend on your organization's policy, the impact of the issue, and other factors. It will also require a thorough and unbiased assessment, sound judgment, and the support from your manager and human resources expert.

No Simple Recipe

There's no simple recipe for progressive discipline. Effective progressive discipline requires the gathering of all pertinent facts, using sound judgment to assess the information, and seeking the advice of your organization's key people, who are usually your manager and human resources expert.

When I started my management journey, I wanted a step-by-step guide to progressive discipline. I wanted a simple cookbook with easy-to-follow recipes that my leadership team could apply in all situations. Since I couldn't find one, I tried to create my own. As my team tackled different performance improvement scenarios, I would document the steps we took in hopes that we would be able to replicate them the next time around. It didn't take me long to figure out that I was wasting my time. In each case, there were many variables that impacted the appropriate course of action. I quickly realized that I would never develop a progressive discipline cookbook that would cover all the necessary recipes.

I put my makeshift cookbook away and focused my energies on understanding people and what inspires, develops, and equips them to achieve excellence. I also developed expertise in my organization's policies, procedures, and philosophy regarding progressive discipline. This philosophy evolved with changes in roles, leadership, human resources experts, and environmental conditions. Over time, I taught managers and supervisors how to apply the progressive discipline process on a case-by-case basis, always starting with gathering the facts.

Gathering the Facts

If you determine that an employee is struggling with performance, customer service, or behavior, start by gathering and evaluating the pertinent facts.

Seek Guidance Immediately

Even if you're a seasoned manager or supervisor, seek guidance. Don't assume that because you have handled similar cases in the past, you're safe to use the same approach. Every situation is different. The specific circumstances of the issue may be different, the organizational climate may have changed, or there may be other nuances that influence the required approach. Leverage your resources. Seek guidance from your direct manager, your human resources expert, or other experts before you have any conversations with employees. Never go it alone.

Act Swiftly

As soon as you identify performance concerns, don't delay in taking action. The sooner you address them, the easier they will be to correct at the lowest possible level. If you wait, the issue will fester and become a much bigger problem requiring more time, energy, and resources to correct.

Uncover the Truth

To determine the appropriate level of discipline, or if any discipline is necessary at all, act with fairness and justice by uncovering the truth.

No Assumptions

Don't start off with assumptions as to people's motives, intentions, or actions. Address each incident and issue on a case-by-case basis and get all the facts.

This is easier said than done. Many of us feel that we're open, fair, and objective. However, we may unknowingly have biases involving many factors, including preconceptions about people based on their past behavior or history. Allowing these prejudices to taint our perspective will interfere with uncovering the truth. Assumptions, whether positive or negative, hamper our ability to act with fairness and justice.

Before you begin to address issues, concerns, and incidents, start without assumptions. Get all facts first and elicit the help of your manager or human resources. Obtaining their support and perspective can help you uphold the integrity of the process, treat employees with fairness, and promote supportive accountability.

Review Performance Data

When you address performance issues, gather and review appropriate performance data and reports. There's always a story behind the numbers. The data doesn't stand alone. Analyze it in light of any mitigating factors and circumstances that may have impacted performance. Uncover the story behind the numbers.

Conduct Investigative Interviews

If the issue involves an alleged incident, interview the person who initially reported the incident as soon as possible. Don't delay in capturing the person's version of the events. With each passing day, the person may forget or unintentionally blur details and facts that may be important in determining the extent and validity of the incident.

As the person relays the information about the incident, maintain neutrality in your facial expressions, body language, the manner in which you frame your questions, and how you respond to the person's version of the events. Listen carefully and ask probing questions to understand the big picture. Gather details and clarify information. Be careful not to imply either agreement or disagreement with the person's perspective.

Close your interview by assuring the person that you will address the concern, but that you won't be able to provide information about how you resolved it because it's confidential. Ask the person to immediately inform you if similar incidents arise in the future so you can address them. This will manage the person's expectations. Before closing the interview, advise the employee that he needs to keep the conversation confidential.

If there are any other parties or witnesses involved, interview them as soon as possible following the same methodology.

Document Immediately

Document the information gathered immediately following each interview. The longer you delay in documenting an interview, the more likely you will forget important facts. If progressive discipline is necessary down the road, strong documentation will be required to support it. Even if the incident may not lead to discipline, file the documentation. If additional concerns arise involving the same employee, this documentation will also help you assess whether discipline is warranted and, if so, at what level. It will also help you identify patterns, should they exist.

> *Documentation Tip: File copies of performance reports and conversation notes in the employee's file.*

Employee Rights to Union Representation

Employees have the right to union representation during interviews for a workplace investigation. These rights, known as Weingarten Rights, are part of U.S. labor law. We won't go into the details of Weingarten Rights or how to apply them, as the law is complex and I am not an attorney. How the law plays out in your workplace depends on many factors.

However, as you conduct investigative interviews to address incidents, issues, and concerns, take these rights into account and consult with your manager and human resources before you proceed. Human resources will usually consult with legal counsel, labor relations, or other experts as appropriate. Seeking guidance is critical to prevent you from unintentionally violating employees' Weingarten Rights.

Factors for Determining the Level of Discipline

Once your investigation is complete, and you have gathered all the pertinent facts, review the documentation. Research and assess the following factors, as your manager and human resources will need the information to determine the level of discipline:

Incident Validity

Do you have documentation that validates that the incident occurred? Don't recommend discipline if you can't prove that the incident is valid.

Employee Failure to Comply with Policies, Procedures, Rules, or Expectations

Do you have documentation that the employee failed to comply with any policies, procedures, rules, or expectations? If yes, which ones and to what extent?

Employee Knowledge of Expectations

Do you have documentation that the employee had already been informed about said policies, procedures, rules, or expectations?

Mitigating Circumstances

Are there any mitigating circumstances that could have affected the employee's ability to meet the expectations? These include chronic or temporary health conditions, personal problems, lack of knowledge, lack of training, lack of resources, and more.

Support

Do you have documentation that you provided adequate support? Do you have documentation that the employee had adequate guidance, tools, training, and resources to meet the policies, procedures, rules, or expectations? If there were mitigating factors, do you have documentation that you provided the employee a reasonable level of support?

Past Performance and Discipline History

How long has the employee been with your company or organization? What type of past performance does the employee's performance record reveal? Has the employee's past performance been stellar, at expected levels, or below expectations? Is there documentation of prior performance issues or disciplinary action? If yes, how many instances are documented? How long ago? At what level? If the employee has prior recorded performance issues or disciplinary action, are the incidents related or similar to the current issue or entirely different issues?

The Seriousness of the Issue or Incident

If the issue or incident was validated, how severe was it? Did the issue or incident pose a risk to the health, safety, and well-being of people? Did it pose a risk of death, injury, or loss of property? Did the issue or incident place the organization at risk of legal consequences, financial loss, audit findings, negative media exposure, or other consequences? Was there an actual negative impact as a result of the issue or incident? If yes, what was it?

The answers to these questions are vital for your organization's designated parties to determine the appropriate level of discipline if any. Depending on the requirements of your organization, there may be other questions you will need to answer. Ask your manager or human resources to clarify your role in this process.

Moving Forward with Discipline

Submit a summary of your findings to your manager and human resources. This summary should include information about the incident, the facts you gathered, and the key factors you assessed. Attach your supporting documentation. This information will provide your manager or human resources a brief, high-level summary they can read quickly, as well as the details necessary for them to decide on the level of discipline.

> *Documentation Tip: File copies of the summary of the findings and supporting documentation in the employee's file. Include copies of all associated emails and other correspondence to your manager and human resources.*

A Word of Caution

In my nearly two decades of experience in performance management, I have seen many leaders at various organizational levels make the same mistake. They work extensively behind the scenes with their employees to the best of their ability, trying to help them improve performance. Some even reach the point of having informal, undocumented, and in-depth weekly meetings with the employee to provide support. The problem arises when these leaders fail to engage their manager and human resources expert early in the process, and performance doesn't improve. They reach out for support when they're so deep into the problem that they're frustrated and desperate for assistance. Many are disheartened to learn that all their work was to no avail. They must start all over at square one because they either failed to progress, to document, or both. Not only is this frustrating for the supervisor, the manager, and human resources, it's a waste of time, energy, and money. Keep your manager and human resources informed as soon as issues arise. It will make your job a lot easier and keep you out of hot water.

In Review

Progressive discipline is a tool to help employees improve performance and behavior through progressive levels of supportive teaching and correction. As you engage in progressive discipline, you may achieve one of three outcomes:

1. The employee succeeds and meets expectations,

2. The employee decides the job isn't a good fit and voluntarily moves on to another role, or

3. You help the employee out the door by progressing through the levels of discipline.

These levels of discipline vary from organization to organization. However, here are five that are commonly used:

1. Verbal warning,

2. Written warning,

3. Suspension,

4. Demotion, and

5. Termination.

There's no simple recipe for the application of the levels of discipline. Effective progressive discipline requires that you gather and assess all pertinent facts and recommend a level if appropriate. This process may require that you or someone else in your organization conduct investigative interviews. Employees have a right to union representation during these types of interviews, and failure to comply with these rights poses a risk to you and your organization. Therefore, it's paramount that you consult your manager and human resources as you work with employees to help them improve their performance. Don't wait to seek their guidance until after an issue escalates or requires an investigation. Reach out to them as soon as you identify concerns so they can guide you through the process.

Putting It into Action

1. Become familiar with your organization's progressive discipline policies, procedures, and approach.

2. Consult with your manager and human resources before engaging in progressive discipline.

3. Document all your actions.

Chapter 12

The Case for Documentation

Documentation applied in the spirit of supportive accountability
promotes a balanced approach to help the employee succeed.

I f it seems that the word "documentation" is redundant throughout this book, it is. This redundancy is intentional. You have probably heard the phrase "Document. Document. Document." This redundancy emphasizes how critical documentation is to the performance management process.

SUPPORTIVE ACCOUNTABILITY
LEADERSHIP™

The Purpose of Documentation

Many leaders view documentation as building a case for disciplinary action. I have often heard leaders say, "I'm documenting him" or "I'm documenting her." This language signals that documentation is being "done to" the employee with the goal of achieving discipline. This approach doesn't align with supportive accountability. While documentation can support discipline, this isn't the primary goal. Discipline should be your last resort in performance management, not your default. Documentation applied in the spirit of supportive accountability promotes a balanced approach to help the employee succeed.

A Basis for Performance Evaluations

When done effectively, documentation provides you a firm foundation from which to write accurate, complete, and fair performance evaluations. If you consistently document the activities in the other six elements of effective performance management—expectations, monitoring, feedback, support, recognition, and accountability—writing the employee's performance evaluation will be much easier for you. On the other hand, having big gaps in your documentation or missing documentation altogether puts you at risk of basing the evaluation solely on what you can remember. Unfortunately, your memory of recent or isolated events can shape your perception of the employee's overall performance throughout the evaluation period.

Inadequate and incomplete documentation hinders your ability to write fair, impartial, and complete performance evaluations. This is a serious matter, as performance evaluations become part of the employee's record. Employees often depend on their performance evaluations to compete for promotions, receive raises and bonuses, land new jobs, or secure other rewards. Doing your due diligence to capture accurate and complete employee performance isn't optional. As a leader, you have the responsibility to do the right thing for each employee. Having solid documentation on which to base the performance evaluation will help you do that.

Supports Disciplinary Action

Effective documentation guides and supports decisions regarding disciplinary action. The goal of documentation isn't to discipline employees, and most employees won't require discipline to meet performance goals or correct deficiencies. In many cases, success can be achieved through a positive and collaborative approach. However, when discipline is necessary, strong documentation will help you capture and assess the key factors for determining the appropriate level. It will help you ensure your actions are objective, just, and fair—based on facts and not on feelings or opinions. When prepared with sound judgment and the counsel of the appropriate experts, documentation will support your actions.

Remember that employees have rights. If they appeal or grieve disciplinary action that you have either recommended or applied, you must be prepared to submit your supporting documentation as evidence that your actions were justified. If you don't have your documentation organized before disciplinary action is applied, you may find yourself frantically scrambling after the fact to gather the necessary records. Not only is this stressful, but it can be detrimental to your reputation and career.

Mitigates Risk

There are no guarantees that you or your organization won't be exposed to grievances, complaints, or lawsuits as a result of the personnel actions you have taken in your leadership role, no matter how diligent you are. However, you can significantly mitigate this risk by operating in an objective, fair, just, and legal manner; seeking guidance from your manager, human resources, and other experts; and documenting all crucial conversations, actions, and decisions. This documentation becomes the evidence you will need to produce.

Document Successes and Challenges

Effective documentation doesn't focus solely on the negative. It provides a continuous, complete, accurate, and objective record. Solid documentation captures the employee's successes and challenges, as well as the support and accountability you have provided.

Best Practices in Documentation

Documentation can be a labor-intensive and draining process when it involves an employee with extensive behavioral or performance challenges. Here are some best practices that can help alleviate the burden:

Exercise Balance

Don't document too much. Don't document too little. Document enough.

When you provide feedback in the spirit of supportive accountability, you have so many informal conversations that it's impractical, ineffective, and unnecessary to document them all. At the same time, you must keep written records of important conversations. The amount of notes you take can vary depending on your preferences, note-taking skills, and the strength of your memory. If you're highly skilled and have a sharp memory, you can jot down a few words during the conversation and use these to type your notes afterward. If you're not confident you will remember all material information, take more notes.

Document for a Total Stranger

Don't document just for yourself. Document for a total stranger, someone you don't know and who is unfamiliar with your people, products, processes, and service. Remember that a neutral third party, who has no history or background regarding the employee or your workplace, may someday read your documentation to determine if the actions you took were appropriate. Document so that this neutral person can get a clear picture of the events and the justification for your actions.

Document Objectively

Document just the facts. Use objective language. Don't include opinions, speculations, or assumptions. Document the employee's specific behaviors, actions, and statements, as well as your own. Sign and date all documentation to capture the chronology of events and indicate that you're the author.

Document Immediately

Documentation must be done immediately.

As soon as the conversation is over, finalize your notes, so they're accurate, complete, concise, and legible. Record the conversation the same day it occurred or the next day at the latest. Waiting longer than this puts you at risk of forgetting important information or inaccurately recalling the details. Incomplete and inaccurate documentation affects your credibility and can place you and your organization at risk, should the employee file a grievance, complaint, or lawsuit.

Document Neatly

If you're a gifted notetaker, you have legible handwriting, and your preliminary notes can stand alone to paint a clear picture for a neutral third party, you don't have to type them. Sign, date, and file them. However, some of us are not this gifted. We either capture a few words here and there, have illegible handwriting, or both. Therefore, we must type our notes so that a neutral third party can understand them.

Simply Document

The biggest problem that many managers and supervisors run into with documentation is not how they document; it's the fact that they don't.

I have seen managers and supervisors work hard to help employees but fail to document. Many were frustrated about the significant time and energy they spent with an employee without experiencing a breakthrough. Without adequate documentation, they were not able to progress. Without progression, employees didn't improve their performance or behavior. Some leaders merely gave up and settled for lackluster performance. Others experienced the negative consequences of their ineffectiveness in employee performance management.

Don't wait until something goes wrong to start documenting. Document consistently.

Find Your Style

You can document using several formats. The key to minimizing the burden is to use a method that works for you. How you document may vary based on your personal preference, your manager's expectations, your organization's professional guidance, the tools that are available to you, and other factors.

Sample Documentation Formats

Here are some sample formats you can use to make your documentation process easier:

Conversation Notes Template

Use word processing software to create a conversation notes template. This template will provide you with a consistent format, which will help a neutral third party follow your written record. It will also speed up your documentation process. Include the following elements in your template to promote a strong audit trail:

- **Header** – The running header contains the subject of the conversation, the employee's name, and the date and time of the conversation. It helps everyone quickly identify the contents of the document and will prove useful when you need to sift through your documentation to support the progressive discipline process.

- **Notes Section** – This is a blank section where you can describe the conversation. Make your description accurate, complete, concise, and neutral.

- **Signature Block** – The signature block provides a space for you to sign and date the document. Underneath your signature, pre-type your first and last name, your title, and the name of your organization. This information identifies you as the author of the notes. By using the complete signature block, you're providing written testimony of the events and conversation. Your organization will be able to use your notes to support performance evaluations and progressive discipline even after you're gone.

- **Footer** – The running footer contains the page number and the total number of pages in the document. This footer is necessary for documents that have multiple pages. If your document is only one page, then the running footer isn't required.

> *Documentation Tip: Refer to Appendix K – Conversation Notes Template. You can create a custom version to meet your needs. File copies of conversation notes in the employee's file.*

Documentation Notebook

Some conversations don't require formal documentation. These can include informal huddles and check-ins, where you're providing routine guidance and instruction. In these instances, you can record the conversation in a notebook for future reference. You can also use a notebook to document formal feedback conversations and investigative interviews if you're skilled at capturing complete, accurate, and legible notes by hand. However, if you're using a notebook to record sensitive conversations, be vigilant about how you secure the information.

Summary Email

You can also document incidents and conversations by sending a summary email to your manager and human resources expert. This email serves two purposes. First, it provides information to your manager and human resources about the event or conversation. Second, it's a quick and easy way to document. Since emails already contain the date and name of the sender, you don't need to sign and date these unless your organization's protocol requires it. Keep in mind that the transmission of sensitive information via email requires adequate network security. Your manager and human resources can provide information about your organization's IT security policies and procedures. If you're allowed to use email to document performance, retain a copy in the employee's file.

Manual Event Log

An event log is a continuous running manual or electronic document where you can capture events and conversations as they occur. Your manual event log can be as simple as a sheet of paper where you enter the date, time, and brief description of incidents, conversations, or events.

> *Documentation Tip: If you use a Manual Event Log (Appendix L), sign and date each entry you make. The appendix provides an example of how to do this.*

Electronic Event Log

Although you can keep a manual log, I recommend you use an electronic event log. Store it in a secure location on your computer network and create a shortcut to it on your desktop. Incorporate the following elements in your electronic event log:

- **Header** – The running header identifies the document as the event log for a particular employee. Example: "Event Log for (Employee Name)."

- **Comments Section** – This is the blank area of the document where you can enter the date, the time, and a summary of the incident, event, or conversation. You can also enter your name.

- **Signature Block** – At the bottom of the page (not in the footer), add a signature block that contains the words "Prepared by," a place for your signature, your printed name, and your title.

- **Footer** – Since the Event Log is a continuous document, it may involve multiple pages. Therefore, add a running footer that contains the actual page number and the total number of pages in the document.

> *Documentation Tip:* See Appendix M – Electronic Event Log. You can maintain this log in your electronic files. You can also print, sign, and transmit this log as needed. Check with your manager and human resources expert whether your organization accepts electronic signatures so that you don't have to print it.

The Performance Documentation Toolkit

To help make the documentation process easier, I developed the Performance Documentation Toolkit. You can download your free copy at http://eepurl.com/don-vj.

Empower Other Leaders to Document

If you supervise other supervisors, provide them with various samples of documentation formats and allow them the freedom to use what works for them. Encourage them to customize the samples as long as they provide adequate information to inform decisions and meet your organization's requirements.

Document with Integrity

Regardless of the format you use, the integrity of your documentation is of utmost importance. Ensure it's accurate, complete, and legible. Proofread your notes before you print, sign, date, and file. If you find yourself needing to produce documentation you don't have for an old event or conversation, don't recreate notes and backdate them. Be honest and let the requestor know you didn't document the event or conversation. Then describe the events or conversation to the best of your recollection, emphasizing that the information is based on memory. Never do anything to bring your integrity into question, as it can affect the credibility of your documentation and your reputation.

Getting Organized

Set up an easy-to-use organizational system to maintain your employee records. If your filing system is too labor-intensive or complicated, chances are you're not going to file your documentation, and this can lead to disaster. Having a simple and well-organized system will allow you to file and retrieve your documentation quickly, which someday may protect you or your organization.

Use standardized categories for the organization and easy retrieval of documents. Here are some examples to get you started:

- Attendance & Punctuality

- Performance Monitoring

- Conferences & Feedback

- Recognition

- Training

- Expectations

- Other

You can use these categories or create your own. You can also determine the category order that will work best for you. The important thing is to categorize your documentation so that you can get to it quickly when you need it. If you find yourself having to document extensively for a particular employee due to attendance, performance, or behavioral issues, you may need to change your categories altogether. For instance, you may categorize by incident, issue, or performance area, depending on the nature and volume of the documentation. You will need to decide what works best depending on the specific situation.

Paper-Based Filing System

For a paper-based filing system, use a folder for each employee and use a consistent naming convention for all your folders. For instance: Last Name, First Name or First Name, Last Name. Use tabs to separate the categories. You can arrange them in order of frequency of use, with the least frequently used at the bottom and the most frequently used on top. You can also arrange them in alphabetical order. Whichever arrangement you use, be consistent with all your employee files for ease and speed of use. If you need to document extensively for a particular employee, you may need to move from a paper folder to one or more binders. If so, use binder labels and tabs for categorization.

Electronic Filing System

For an electronic filing system, create a structure that uses electronic folders and subfolders to keep the categories neatly organized. As with a paper-based system, be consistent with your naming conventions and categorization.

Hybrid Filing System

You can also use a hybrid filing system that combines both electronic and paper folders and files. However, it's best to leverage technology as much as possible. It's the most eco-friendly, efficient, and cost-effective approach to records management. When you store your electronic files in your company's secure network, you can retrieve them from any computer that has connectivity and access. If set up correctly, when you move from one office to another within the same organization due to internal office moves, lateral transfers, or promotions, you won't need to deal with paper files. Likewise, when the document destruction due date arrives, you're able to electronically shred your documents, which is far less time-consuming and labor-intensive than physical shredding. If your organization has strong electronic records security policies and you follow them, an electronic system safeguards your records more than paper-based files.

Safeguard Your Documentation

As a supervisor, you're entrusted with highly confidential and sensitive information. Safeguard your documentation from unauthorized access. Keep physical documents under lock and key and maintain electronic records in a secure network environment. Your organization will have specific policies, procedures, and protocols for protecting sensitive and confidential information. Become knowledgeable in these and adhere to them.

Human Resources Policies and Procedures

As a manager or supervisor, you must develop a strong knowledge of your organization's policies, procedures, and protocols for documentation and comply with them. Seek guidance from your direct supervisor and human resources experts to meet these expectations.

Maintaining strong documentation can be taxing. However, these documentation best practices can help alleviate the burden. Remember, there may come a time when you need your documentation for appeals, grievances, hearings, or even in your defense. You won't always need to use your documentation for these types of events. Often your records will be uneventful and will gather dust until it's time to purge them in alignment with your organization's document retention and destruction policies. However, if the time comes when you find yourself needing to support your actions, you will be relieved when you're able to demonstrate your due diligence.

In Review

Documentation isn't a luxury. It's a mandatory and crucial part of your job as a manager or supervisor. Effective documentation serves as evidence in the performance management process. It provides a sound basis for fair, objective, and accurate performance evaluations; supports disciplinary action when necessary; and mitigates risk to you and the organization.

Putting It into Action

Get organized for documentation efficiency:

1. Find out your organization's policies and procedures for performance management documentation.

2. Decide on the type of organization system for your employee files—paper-based, electronic, or hybrid.

3. For consistency, determine which categories you will need for each employee folder.

4. Determine how you will safeguard your documentation.

Chapter 13
Final Wrap Up: Practical Application

*Effective leadership is paramount for creating a supportive environment
that engages employees and promotes strong performance.*

The Supportive Accountability Leadership Model isn't a cookie-cutter approach. It's a simple, yet powerful framework that will help you engage employees and improve performance. At the core of the model is supportive accountability, which blends supportive supervision and accountability to ignite strong performance.

The Four Leadership Styles of Supportive Accountability™

The model frames performance management using four basic leadership styles.

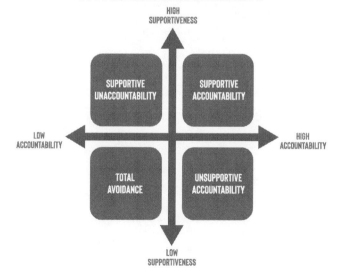

**FOUR LEADERSHIP STYLES OF
SUPPORTIVE ACCOUNTABILITY™**

189

1. ***Unsupportive Accountability*** is characterized by high levels of accountability and low levels of support. In extreme cases of this approach, leaders apply a high degree of accountability but fail to provide the emotional and material support employees need to be successful.

2. ***Supportive Unaccountability*** is demonstrated by high levels of support and low levels of accountability. Leaders who operate with a high degree of supportive unaccountability tend to worry too much about being liked and making employees happy.

3. ***Total Avoidance*** is the absence of both support and accountability. This is a hands-off approach, where leaders relinquish their responsibility to lead, guide, inspire, and hold themselves and their employees accountable for meeting organizational goals.

4. ***Supportive Accountability*** is the most effective of the four performance management styles. It's exemplified by a high level of supportiveness complemented by a high level of accountability. Effective leaders gauge each situation and provide the right amount of support and accountability based on the needs of the individual employee, the facts involved, environmental conditions, and other factors.

These four leadership styles are not about personality; they're about the approach.

The Seven Elements of Strong Performance Management

The Supportive Accountability Leadership Model is comprised of the seven elements of strong performance management—expectations, monitoring, feedback, support, recognition, accountability, and documentation.

SUPPORTIVE ACCOUNTABILITY LEADERSHIP™

Let's review the seven elements.

Element 1 – Expectations

Expectations are the foundation for achieving success. They give direction and focus. Without clear expectations, employees are aiming in the dark and their opportunities for success are diminished. Chapter 3 provides information about goals and expectations and shows you how to develop an Expectations Packet.

Element 2 – Monitoring

Monitoring is the act of measuring, observing, and reviewing performance. It focuses employees on what matters. Align your monitoring activities with established, known, and objective performance expectations. Refer to Chapter 4 for an overview of the essential principles of performance monitoring. Chapter 5 provides information on how to monitor customer service.

Element 3 – Feedback

Performance feedback lets employees know whether or not they're on target in meeting expectations, goals, and objectives. When provided through a collaborative, two-way conversation, feedback can improve performance. Chapter 6 outlines best practices in performance feedback, and Chapter 7 focuses on leading effective performance improvement conversations.

Element 4 – Support

To perform at their best, employees need support. Support comes in many forms, including tools, equipment, and supplies; training; access to information; individualized referrals for assistance with personal problems; and more. As a leader, you're the most important source of support for the employees on your team. The magnitude of your influence can't be overemphasized. For you to adequately identify the support needs of your employees, you must establish a strong supervisor-employee relationship. Chapter 2 provides you with information on how to do this. Chapter 8 focuses on several critical support factors that employees may need to be successful.

Element 5 – Recognition

Employee recognition lets employee know that their contributions towards the goals of the organization are acknowledged and appreciated. It also reinforces expectations. In the Supportive

Accountability Leadership Model, employee recognition is defined as "showing employees they're appreciated and shining a light on great performance." This simple definition focuses on creating a culture of appreciation. Effective recognition is timely, specific, meaningful, and frequent. Remember that each employee is unique. Find out how she needs and wants to be recognized. Chapter 9 provides some ideas on the types of recognition you can use.

Element 6 – Accountability

As a leader, you're responsible for holding yourself and employees accountable for meeting performance goals and objectives. The 4 P's of Accountability is a framework within the Supportive Accountability Leadership Model that can help you promote accountability. This framework consists of four principles.

1. **People -** People are your organization's most important resource. They need to feel safe, valued, and cared about as you promote accountability.

2. **Purpose -** Accountability starts with purpose. In Supportive Accountability Leadership, the goal of accountability isn't to punish, but rather to create a supportive work environment where employees can thrive and drive performance.

3. **Performance -** Accountability promotes performance. Effective supervisors manage performance with a balanced approach of support and accountability to move the dial in the right direction. They achieve and sustain great performance by simultaneously creating a great work environment and continuously focusing on performance.

4. **Progression -** Progression is the act of moving forward through continuous improvement until you achieve the desired performance outcomes. For accountability to advance performance, use progression.

Chapter 10 provides more information on the 4 P's of Accountability, and Chapter 11 contains an overview of the progressive discipline process.

Element 7– Documentation

Adequate documentation is critical in the performance management process. It serves as evidence that you met your responsibility to manage employee performance and that you did so in the spirit of supportive accountability. When done correctly, and with the guidance of your manager, human resources, or other person designated by your organization, it mitigates risk to you and your organization. Chapter 12 contains suggestions for organizing your documentation, as well as several documentation templates. You can also download your free copy of the Performance Documentation Toolkit at http://eepurl.com/don-vj.

The seven elements are not necessarily sequential and are all interconnected. Depending on the situation, leaders may use two or more of these simultaneously. Let's review how you can apply these seven elements with a new employee, a strong-performing employee, and an employee who is struggling to meet performance expectations.

Applying the Seven Elements

Here are some examples of how you can apply the seven elements with new, strong-performing, and struggling employees.

New Employee

- **Expectations** – Facilitate a one-on-one introductory meeting with the new employee. Issue and review the Expectations Packet. Find out what the employee needs and expects from you. Keep in mind that the employee may be nervous. Use the first meeting to break the ice, establish rapport, and put the employee at ease. Let him know that your goal is to provide him the support he needs to be successful.

- **Support** – Have a checklist of the equipment, tools, and supplies the new employee will need and provide these to him upon arrival. Immediately develop and implement a training plan for the employee to master his role. Check in with the employee frequently to ensure he has the necessary resources to succeed.

- **Monitoring** – Establish a monitoring plan for the new employee to ensure you're measuring, observing, and reviewing performance. Remember that the employee is on a learning curve. Be patient in the beginning as the employee acclimates to his new environment and role.

- **Feedback** – Consider biweekly conferences with the new employee during his first few months in the position, as he will be on a learning curve. You can reduce the frequency to monthly as his need for guidance decreases. Use these conferences to teach, build trust, and establish a strong supervisor-employee relationship. The approach you take in providing initial feedback will lay the foundation for your supervisor-employee relationship. Make it a positive one.

- **Recognition** – During his initial learning phase, the new employee needs frequent praise, acknowledgment, and recognition for progress in learning his new role. He's still trying to make sense of his environment, his relationship with you, and how well he's doing. Intentionally look for opportunities to acknowledge progress and performance in meaningful ways.

- **Accountability** – Your responsibility is to manage performance in the spirit of supportive accountability. His role is to use your support and guidance to meet performance expectations.

- **Documentation** – Document. Chapter 13 provides several templates that can make documentation much easier.

Strong-Performing Employee

- **Expectations** – Reissue and review the Expectations Packet at least annually with your entire team. Reinforce expectations for the individual employee through positive feedback and employee recognition.

- **Monitoring** – Continue to monitor performance for strong-performing employees. Since the employee is performing well, your monitoring frequency can be monthly.

- **Feedback** – Hold regularly scheduled one-on-one conferences with the employee. When you assign a new role or project to the employee, schedule status check meetings to provide input, support, and guidance. Offer plenty of on-the-spot positive feedback. It's easy to neglect strong-performing employees because they usually get the job done without intervention. However, continue to engage them and provide them with a motivating work environment.

- **Support** – Continue to ask strong-performing employees about their support needs. Just because employees are doing well doesn't mean that they have everything they need. Some high-performing employees may perform well even without adequate resources, but they may experience frustration.

- **Recognition** – Reward the employee for exceptional performance. Consider giving formal recognition.

- **Accountability** – Hold the employee accountable for meeting performance goals. Hold yourself accountable for providing support.

- **Documentation** – Document.

Struggling Employee

- **Expectations** – When an employee is facing challenges, start by reviewing and clarifying the relevant expectations during a one-on-one, two-way conversation. Ensure the employee understands the expectations and that you understand what the employee needs from you.

- **Monitoring** – Increase the monitoring frequency in the areas that the employee is struggling in. This will help you prepare for feedback conversations and identify potential support needs. Continue to monitor other vital areas.

- **Feedback** – Provide early intervention and engage the employee in performance improvement conversations. If possible, discuss performance improvement outside of the recurring individual conference. Continue to provide positive feedback through individual conferences, on-the-spot feedback, and unplanned check-ins.

- **Support** – During your feedback conversations, ask the employee what he needs to be successful. Some employees may not realize what they need; therefore, conduct an assessment. Does the employee have the proper tools, equipment, supplies, and training? Does he know how to access essential resources and information? Does the employee need resources to overcome an addiction, mental health need, domestic violence, disability, workplace injury, or other sensitive situation? Addressing the employee's support needs is vital to helping him achieve success.

- **Recognition** – Although the employee is struggling in one area, he may be doing well in another. Don't be afraid to recognize and praise him for what he's doing well. Recognition is also a form of support. This positive acknowledgment could provide him with the emotional boost to help him overcome his challenges.

- **Accountability** – If necessary, apply progressive discipline with the advice of human resources or other key people in your organization.

- **Documentation** – Document.

Prepare for the performance improvement conversation using Appendix J, Performance Improvement Conversation Plan.

A Strong Supervisor-Employee Relationship is the Key

A strong supervisor-employee relationship is the foundation of the Supportive Accountability Leadership Model. This relationship is the most important form of support you can provide each employee. You can establish and nurture it using three pillars—trust, effective communication, and empowerment.

Effective leadership is paramount for creating a supportive environment that engages employees and promotes strong performance. Supportive Accountability Leadership isn't about personality. It's about the approach. Supportive accountability is a skill that can be learned and refined. As a leader, you can actively choose to manage performance in the spirit of supportive accountability. This choice will have a significant impact on your workplace, the people you lead, and the type of performance you will inspire.

A Friendly Request

Thank you for reading this book. I hope you enjoyed it. I would greatly appreciate you providing an honest review of this book at LeadershipStrength.com/bookreview. It will only take a couple of minutes of your time, and you can do so anonymously.

Your review is important and supports the work that I do to create great workplaces and improve performance. Thank you for your time!

Regards,
Sylvia Melena

Free Copy of the Performance Documentation Toolkit

Lighten the burden of documenting employee performance. Download your free copy of the Performance Documentation Toolkit. It will make documenting employee performance easier. Get more information about this handy toolkit at http://eepurl.com/don-vj.

About the Author

Sylvia Melena is the architect of the Supportive Accountability Leadership™ Model. She's also the Founder and CEO of Melena Consulting Group, a leadership and management consulting and training company in San Diego County, California. The company helps businesses and organizations strengthen their leadership and management capabilities, create great workplaces, and improve performance.

Sylvia has a Master of Arts in Leadership and Organizational Studies and fourteen years of experience in middle, senior, and executive management. She has led individuals, small teams, and workforces of up to 300 employees into successful performance improvement. Sylvia has also coached, developed, and trained hundreds of emerging and seasoned managers and supervisors.

For more information about Sylvia or her company, please visit LeadershipStrength.com. You can connect with Sylvia at smelena@melenaconsulting.com.

Other Resources

Melena Consulting Group provides leadership, management, and workplace assessments and training solutions. We specialize in:

- Leadership Development,

- Employee Engagement,

- Performance Management, and

- Culture Change.

For more information, please visit us at LeadershipStrength.com.

Appendix A
Acknowledgment of Receipt

I acknowledge that I have received a copy of the following policies, procedures, and expectations; that my supervisor has reviewed them with me; that I have been given an opportunity to ask questions; and that I understand them.

- YouthZone Employee Handbook dated 00/00/00.
- YouthZone Attendance Policy dated 00/00/00.
- YouthZone Customer Service Expectations dated 00/00/00.
- Youth Employment Program Performance Expectations dated 00/00/00.

_____   _____

Employee Signature   Date

_____

Printed Name and Title of Employee

Notes:
- *The itemized list is for illustration purposes only.*
- *These are not recommended policies, procedures, or expectations. They were selected arbitrarily.*

Appendix B
Monthly Program Performance Report

Youth Employment Program
Monthly Program Performance Report

Report Month: May 0000

Unit No.	Placed in 30	Total Placed	% Placed in 30 Days	# Retained Jobs at 90 Days	# at 90 Days from Placement	% Met 90 Day Retention
Unit 10	44	49	90%	40	53	75%
Unit 20	43	50	86%	35	49	71%
Unit 30	48	52	92%	42	52	81%
Unit 40	42	48	88%	40	51	78%
Unit 50	41	49	84%	34	50	68%
Cumulative	218	248	88%	191	255	75%
		GOAL:	90%		GOAL:	75%

Notes:

- *Vic supervises Unit 30.*

- *Data on this table is for illustration purposes only. Numbers were selected arbitrarily.*

- *These are not recommended benchmarks or actual figures.*

Appendix C
Monthly Unit Performance Report

Youth Employment Program
Monthly Unit Performance Report

Unit: 30
Supervisor: Vic C.
Report Month: May 0000

Unit No.	Placed in 30	Total Placed	% Placed in 30 Days	# Retained Jobs at 90 Days	# at 90 Days from Placement	% Met 90 Day Retention
31	6	7	86%	6	8	75%
32	7	8	88%	6	8	75%
33	6	6	100%	6	7	86%
34	8	9	89%	6	8	75%
35	7	7	100%	6	7	86%
36	6	7	86%	6	7	86%
37	8	8	100%	6	7	86%
Cumulative	48	52	92%	42	52	81%
		GOAL:	90%		GOAL:	75%

Notes:
- *Counselor 37 is Mary.*
- *Data on this table is for illustration purposes only. Numbers were selected arbitrarily.*
- *These are not recommended benchmarks or actual figures.*

211

Appendix D
Employee Performance Trend Report

Youth Employment Program
Employee Performance Trend Report
Month: May 0000
Counselor: 37
Counselor Name: Mary J

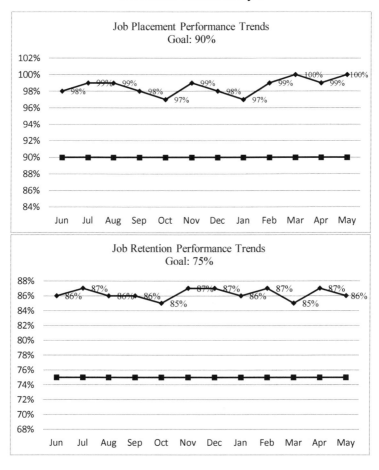

Notes:

- *Data on this table is for illustration purposes only. Numbers were selected arbitrarily.*
- *These are not recommended benchmarks or actual figures.*

Appendix E
Customer Satisfaction Survey

Dear YouthZone Participant:

We value your opinion and strive to serve you with excellence. Please take a few minutes to tell us about your experience with us. We will use this information to improve our services.

Today's date: _____

Date you received the service: _____

Name of the person who served you (if known):

_____

Please rate your experience. For each of the four statements below, please put an "x" in the box that best describes your agreement with the statement.

		1 Strongly Disagree	2 Disagree	3 Neutral	4 Agree	5 Strongly Agree
1	I was treated professionally.					
2	I was served on time.					
3	I received answers to all my questions.					
4	I received all the help I needed.					

In the space below, please tell us more about your experience:

Name: _____   Telephone Number: _____

Do you wish to be contacted about your experience (please circle one):   Yes   No

Notes:
- *Questions and responses are for illustration purposes only.*
- *These are not recommended questions or responses.*

Appendix F
Unit Customer Satisfaction Report

Youth Employment Program
Unit Customer Satisfaction Report
Report Date: 00/00/00
Report Period: 00/00/00 – 00/00/00

Unit: 30
Supervisor: Vic C.
Report Month: May 0000

Counselor	Professionalism	Promptness	Responsiveness	Assistance
31	4.0	4.5	4.3	4.3
32	5.0	4.8	5.0	5.0
33	4.8	4.9	4.7	4.8
34	5.0	5.0	4.9	5.0
35	4.6	4.3	4.0	4.0
36	4.0	4.5	4.3	4.4
37	2.6	4.6	3.8	4.0
Average	4.3	4.7	4.4	4.5
Goal	4.0	4.0	4.0	4.0

Notes:

- *Counselor 37 is Mary.*
- *Data on this table is for illustration purposes only. Numbers were selected arbitrarily.*
- *These are not recommended benchmarks or actual figures.*

Appendix G
Employee Customer Satisfaction Report

Youth Employment Program
Employee Customer Satisfaction Report
Report Date: 00/00/00
Report Period: 00/00/00 – 00/00/00

Counselor Number: 37
Counselor Name: Mary J.

Ratings:

Survey #	Professionalism	Promptness	Responsiveness	Assistance
1	4.0	4	4	4
2	1	5	3	3
3	3	5	4	5
4	2	4	4	4
5	3	5	4	4
Average	2.6	4.6	3.8	4.0
Goal	4.0	4.0	4.0	4.0

Comments:

Survey #	Comments
1	**Comments:** Mary was great. She got me into a job really fast. **Phone Call Welcomed:** Yes
2	**Comments:** I was helped quickly but I felt rushed. She was just trying to get me out of the office. She didn't listen to me and she made rude comments. **Phone Call Welcomed:** Yes
3	**Comments:** None **Phone Call Welcomed:** No
4	**Comments:** None **Phone Call Welcomed:** No
5	**Comments:** None **Phone Call Welcomed:** No

Notes:

- *Data on this table is for illustration purposes only. Numbers were selected arbitrarily.*
- *These are not recommended benchmarks or actual figures.*

Appendix H
Customer Interaction Observation Tool

Observation Date: _____

Observation #: _____

Employee Name: _____

Type of Customer Interaction: _____

Criteria Observed	Criteria Met?			Comments Section
Promptness	**Yes**	**No**	**N/A**	**Comments**
Counselor greeted the customer by the appointment start time.				
First Impressions	**Yes**	**No**	**N/A**	**Comments**
Counselor was dressed professionally.				
Counselor smiled.				
Counselor greeted the customer in a friendly manner.				
Identity and Contact Information Verification	**Yes**	**No**	**N/A**	**Comments**
Counselor verified youth identity using three pieces of information.				
Counselor confirmed current address, phone number, and email address.				
Interaction	**Yes**	**No**	**N/A**	**Comments**
Counselor used a respectful tone of voice.				
Counselor used respectful body language.				
Counselor used respectful verbal language.				
Counselor listened to the customer.				
Counselor asked clarifying questions, if necessary.				
Counselor adequately answered the customer's questions and concerns.				
Counselor demonstrated knowledge in providing information.				
Problem Resolution	**Yes**	**No**	**N/A**	**Comments**
Counselor solved the customer's problem, took appropriate action, or referred the customer to appropriate resource.				

Reviewer Printed Name: _____

Signature: _____ Date: _____

Notes:

- *Tool is for illustration purposes only. Criteria were selected arbitrarily.*
- *These are not recommended criteria.*

221

Appendix I
Observations Summary Report

Date: _____

Employee Name: _____

Criteria Observed	Criteria Met?			Comments Section
	Yes	No	N/A	
Promptness	#1	#2	#3	**Comments**
Counselor greeted the customer by the appointment start time.				
First Impressions	#1	#2	#3	**Comments**
Counselor was dressed professionally.				
Counselor smiled.				
Counselor greeted the customer in a friendly manner.				
Identity and Contact Information Verification	#1	#2	#3	**Comments**
Counselor verified youth identity using three pieces of information.				
Counselor confirmed current address, phone number, and email address.				
Interaction	#1	#2	#3	**Comments**
Counselor used a respectful tone of voice.				
Counselor used respectful body language.				
Counselor used a respectful verbal language.				
Counselor listened to the customer.				
Counselor asked clarifying questions, if necessary.				
Counselor adequately answered the customer's questions and concerns.				
Counselor demonstrated knowledge in providing information.				
Problem Resolution	#1	#2	#3	**Comments**
Counselor solved the customer's problem, took appropriate action, or referred the customer to appropriate resource.				

Scoring

A - Total "Yes"	B – Total "No"	C – Total "N/A"	D – Subtotal (A + B + C)	% Criteria Met (A+C)/D

Reviewer Printed Name: _____

Signature: _____ Date: _____

Notes: Tool is for illustration purposes only. These are not recommended criteria.

Notes: Tool is for illustration purposes only. These are not recommended criteria.

223

Appendix J

Performance Improvement Conversation Plan

Considerations	Plan
On what date and time do you plan to meet? Consider timing.	
Where do you plan to meet? Consider privacy and comfort.	
What is the single issue you want to address? Don't overwhelm the employee.	
How can you start the conversation on a positive note?	
How will you explain the purpose of the conversation?	
What performance goals/expectations do you want to review with the employee?	
What specific examples will you provide the employee about how he/she is performing relative to the goals/expectations?	
What questions will you use to ask the employee for his/her perspective and input? Examples: • What are your successes? • What are your challenges? • What support do you need to be successful? • How can I better support you?	
What support can you offer the employee to help him/her succeed? Examples: • Job shadowing other employees • Mentoring • Targeted training • Other Critical Support Factors	
What measurable goals will you propose to evaluate employee progress towards improvement?	
What date and time is the follow-up meeting to evaluate the employee's progress?	

Note: Tool is for illustration purposes only

Appendix K
Conversation Notes Template

Conversation with *(Employee Name)* About *(Incident Name)*
(Date), (Time), (Location)

(Type notes here)

Signature | 00/00/00

Full Name, Title | Date
Organization Name

Page 1 of 2

Note: Tool is for illustration purposes only.

Appendix L
Manual Event Log

Event Log for *(Employee Name)*

00/00/00 – *(Enter your manual notes here.)* – Vic C.

Note: Tool is for illustration purposes only.

Appendix M
Electronic Event Log

Event Log for *(Employee Name)*

00/00/00 – (Enter your manual notes here.) – Vic C.

Prepared by:

Signature
_____

Full Name, Title
Organization Name

Endnotes

Chapter 1 – The Heart of Supportive Accountability

No notes

Chapter 2 – The Art of Supportive Leadership

1   Florence Stinglhamber et al., "Employees' Organizational Identification and Affective Organizational Commitment: An Integrative Approach," *PLoS ONE* 10, no. 4 (2015): 1–23. https://doi.org/10.1371/journal.pone.0123955. Creative Commons License: https://creativecommons.org/licenses/by/4.0/.

2   Ishfaq Ahmed et al., "A Literary Look at Outcomes of Support at Work," *Research Journal of Applied Sciences, Engineering and Technology* 5, no. 12 (2013): 3444–3449, http://maxwellsci.com/print/rjaset/v5-3444-3449.pdf. Creative Commons License: https://creativecommons.org/licenses/by/3.0/.

3   Florence Stinglhamber et al., "Employees' Organizational Identification," 1–23.

4   J.D. Tony Carter, "Managers Empowering Employees," *American Journal of Economics and Business Administration* 1, no. 2 (2009): 41–46, http://thescipub.com/PDF/ajebasp.2009.41.46.pdf. Creative Commons License: https://creativecommons.org/licenses/by/4.0/.

5   Cody Logan Chullen, "How Does Supervisor Burnout Affect Leader-Member Exchange? A Dyadic Perspective," *International Business & Economics Research Journal* 13, no. 5 (2014): 1113–1126, https://doi.org/10.19030/iber.v13i5.8777. Creative Commons License: https://creativecommons.org/licenses/by/3.0/.

6   Janine Victor and Crystal C. Hoole. "The Influence of Organisational Rewards on Workplace Trust and Work Engagement," *SA Journal of Human Resource Management* 1, no. 0, (2017): 1–14, https://sajhrm.co.za/index.php/sajhrm/article/view/853. Creative Commons License: https://creativecommons.org/licenses/by/4.0/.

7   Janine Victor and Crystal C. Hoole, "The Influence of Organisational Rewards," 1–14.

8   Schalk W. Grobler and Yvonne du Plessis, "Requisite Leader Behavioural Competencies for Sustainable Organisational Performance," *Acta Commercii* 16, no. 1 (2016): 1–8. http://dx.doi.org/10.4102/ac.v16i1.347. Creative Commons License: https://creativecommons.org/licenses/by/4.0/.

9   Cody Logan Chullen, "How Does Supervisor Burnout," 1113–1126.

10   Jing Qian, Bin Wang, Zhuo Han, and Baihe Song, "Ethical Leadership, Leader-Member Exchange and Feedback Seeking: a Double-Moderated Mediation Model of Emotional Intelligence and Work-Unit Structure," *Frontiers in Psychology* 8, no. 1174 (2017): 1–11, https://doi.org/10.3389/fpsyg.2017.01174. Creative Commons License: https://creativecommons.org/licenses/by/4.0/.

11   Tajammal Hussain and Sheikh Sana ur Rehman, "Do Human Resource Management Practices Inspire Employees' Retention?, " *Research Journal of Applied Sciences, Engineering and Technology* 6, no. 19 (2013): 3625–3633, http://maxwellsci.com/print/rjaset/v6-3625-3633.pdf. Creative Commons License: https://creativecommons.org/licenses/by/3.0/.

12   J.D. Tony Carter, "Managers Empowering Employees," 41–46.

13   Tajammal Hussain and Sheikh Sana ur Rehman, "Do Human Resource Management," 3625–3633.

14   Haleema Zia, Hafiz Muhammad Ishaq, Salma Zahir, and Faiz Ahmed, "To Investigate the Impact of Training, Employee Empowerment and Organizational Climate on Job Performance," *Research Journal of Applied Sciences, Engineering and Technology* 7, no. 22 (2014): 4832–4837, http://www.maxwellsci.com/msproof. php?doi=rjaset.7.872. Creative Commons License: https://creativecommons. org/licenses/by/3.0/.

15   Kartinah Ayupp and Then Hsiao Chung, "Empowerment: Hotel Employees' Perspective," 561–575.

16   Janine Victor and Crystal C. Hoole, "The Influence of Organisational Rewards," 1–14.

17   Janine Krüger and Chantal Rootman, "How Do Small Business Managers Influence Employee Satisfaction and Commitment?," *Acta Commercii* 10, no. 1 (2010): 59–72, http://www.actacommercii.co.za/index.php/acta/article/ viewFile/114/114. Creative Commons License: https://creativecommons.org/ licenses/by/4.0/.

18   Kartinah Ayupp and Then Hsiao Chung, "Empowerment: Hotel Employees' Perspective," *Journal of Industrial Engineering and Management* 3, no. 3 (2010): 561–575, http://www.jiem.org/index.php/jiem/article/view/166/81. Creative Commons License: https://creativecommons.org/licenses/by/3.0/.

19   Kartinah Ayupp and Then Hsiao Chung, "Empowerment: Hotel Employees' Perspective," 561–575.

20   J.D. Tony Carter, "Managers Empowering Employees," 41–46.

21   J.D. Tony Carter, "Managers Empowering Employees," 41–46.

22   Ishfaq Ahmed et al., "A Literary Look," 3444–3449.

23   J.D. Tony Carter, "Managers Empowering Employees," 41–46.

Chapter 3 – Expectations that Inspire

24   Nico W. Van Yperen, Monica Blaga, and Tom Postmes, "A Meta-Analysis of Self-Reported Achievement Goals and Nonself-Report Performance across Three Achievement Domains (Work, Sports, and Education)," *PloS ONE* 9, no. 4 (2014): 1–16, https://doi.org/10.1371/journal.pone.0093594. Creative Commons License: https://creativecommons.org/licenses/by/4.0/. This book uses the terms **self-development goals** and **peer comparison goals** instead of those used in the research. The researchers refer to these two types of goals as **mastery-approach (MAp) goals** and **performance-approach (PAp) goals**, respectively.

25   Nico W. Van Yperen, Monica Blaga, and Tom Postmes, "A Meta-Analysis," 1–16.

26   Nico W. Van Yperen, Monica Blaga, and Tom Postmes, "A Meta-Analysis," 1–16.

27   Monica Blaga and Nico W. Van Yperen, "Easy and Difficult Performance-Approach Goals: Their Moderating Effect on the Link Between Task Interest and Performance Attainment," *Psychologica Belgica* 48, no. 2–3 (2008): 93–107, http://doi.org/10.5334/pb-48-2-3-93. Creative Commons License: https://creativecommons.org/licenses/by/4.0/.

28   Monica Blaga and Nico W. Van Yperen, "Easy and Difficult Performance-Approach Goals," 93–107.

29   Nico W. Van Yperen, Monica Blaga, and Tom Postmes, "A Meta-Analysis," 1–16.

Chapter 4 – Monitoring: Focusing on What Matters

30   Schalk W. Grobler and Yvonne du Plessis, "Requisite Leader Behavioural Competencies for Sustainable Organisational Performance," *Acta Commercii* 16, no. 1 (2016): 1–8, http://dx.doi.org/10.4102/ac.v16i1.347. Creative Commons License: https://creativecommons.org/licenses/by/4.0/.

31   Mihaela Rus. "Transformational Leadership Type in Public and Private Organizations" *EIRP Proceedings* 7, no. 1 (2012): 588–594, http://www.proceedings. univ-danubius.ro/index.php/eirp/article/view/1246/1225. Creative Commons License: https://creativecommons.org/licenses/by/4.0/.

32   M. Rosario Perello-Marin and Gabriela Ribes-Giner, "Identifying a Guiding List of High Involvement Practices in Human Resource Management," *WPOM-Working Papers on Operations Management* 5, no. 1 (2014): 31–47, https://polipapers. upv.es/index.php/WPOM/article/view/1495. Creative Commons License: https://creativecommons.org/licenses/by/4.0/.

33   Monica Blaga and Nico W. Van Yperen, "Easy and Difficult Performance-Approach Goals: Their Moderating Effect on the Link Between Task Interest and Performance Attainment," *Psychologica Belgica* 48, no. 2–3 (2008): 93–107, http://doi.org/10.5334/pb-48-2-3-93. Creative Commons License: https:// creativecommons.org/licenses/by/4.0/. Nico W. Van Yperen, Monica Blaga, and Tom Postmes, "A Meta-Analysis of Self-Reported Achievement Goals and Nonself-Report Performance across Three Achievement Domains (Work, Sports, and Education)," *PloS ONE* 9, no. 4 (2014): 1 – 16. https://doi.org/10.1371/ journal.pone.0093594. Creative Commons License: https://creativecommons. org/licenses/by/4.0/.

Chapter 5 – Measuring Customer Service

34   Richard M. Heiberger and Naomi B. Robbins, "Design of Diverging Stacked Bar Charts for Likert Scales and Other Applications," *Journal of Statistical Software* 57, no. 1 (2014): 1–32. https://www.jstatsoft.org/article/view/2132. Creative Commons License: https://creativecommons.org/licenses/by/3.0/.

35   Richard M. Heiberger and Naomi B. Robbins, "Design of Diverging," 1–32.

36   Isac Florin Lucian, Rusu Sergiu, and Cureteanu Radu Silviu, "Problems in Measuring Customer Satisfaction," *Analele Universităţii Constantin Brâncuşi din Târgu Jiu: Seria Economie* 2, no. 4 (2012): 23–25. http://www.utgjiu.ro/revista/ ec/pdf/2012-04.II/3_Isac%20Florin,%20Rusu%20Segiu%20,Cureteanu%20 Radu%201.pdf. Creative Commons License: https://creativecommons.org/ licenses/by/4.0/

37   Isac Florin Lucian, Rusu Sergiu, and Cureteanu Radu Silviu, "Problems in Measuring Customer Satisfaction," 23–25.

38   Wendi Brick, interview by Sylvia Melena, November 7, 2017. I interviewed Wendi Brick, President & CEO of Customer Service Advantage, Inc. and author of *The Science of Service: Six Essential Elements for Creating a Culture of Service in the Public Sector.* Wendi's life work is advancing world-class customer service in the public sector. For more information, please visit www.thecsaedge.com.

39   Wendi Brick, November 7, 2017.

40   Wendi Brick, November 7, 2017.

41   Wendi Brick, November 7, 2017.

42   Wendi Brick, November 7, 2017.

43   Wendi Brick, November 7, 2017.

44   Wendi Brick, November 7, 2017.

45   Wendi Brick, November 7, 2017.

46   Wendi Brick, November 7, 2017.

Chapter 6 – Best Practices in Performance Feedback

47   Jing Qian, Bin Wang, Zhuo Han, and Baihe Song, "Ethical Leadership, Leader-Member Exchange and Feedback Seeking: a Double-Moderated Mediation Model of Emotional Intelligence and Work-Unit Structure," *Frontiers in Psychology* 8, no. 1174 (2017): 1–11, https://doi.org/10.3389/fpsyg.2017.01174. Creative Commons License: https://creativecommons.org/licenses/by/4.0/.

Chapter 7 – Leading Performance Improvement Conversations

No notes.

Chapter 8 – Critical Support Factors that Unleash Performance

48   Schalk W. Grobler and Yvonne du Plessis, "Requisite Leader Behavioural Competencies for Sustainable Organisational Performance," *Acta Commercii* 16, no. 1 (2016): 1–8, http://dx.doi.org/10.4102/ac.v16i1.347. Creative Commons License: https://creativecommons.org/licenses/by/4.0/.

49   Haleema Zia et al., "To Investigate the Impact of Training, Employee Empowerment and Organizational Climate on Job Performance," *Research Journal of Applied Sciences, Engineering and Technology* 7, no. 22 (2014): 4832–4837. http://www.maxwellsci.com/msproof.php?doi=rjaset.7.872. Creative Commons License: https://creativecommons.org/licenses/by/3.0/.

50   Haleema Zia et al., "To Investigate the Impact of Training, 4832–4837.

51   Barbara Greenstein, interview by Sylvia Melena, May 26, 2017. I interviewed Barbara Greenstein, Principal of Human Resource Prescriptions, LLC. Barbara is a performance improvement specialist providing proven and creative ways to improve human performance in the workplace. She offers Ramp Up™ Your Performance to help companies make the shift from traditional training to performance interventions. For more information, please visit http://www.hrxi.com/.

52   Barbara Greenstein, May 26, 2017.

53   Barbara Greenstein, May 26, 2017.

54   Barbara Greenstein, May 26, 2017.

55   Haleema Zia et al., "To Investigate the Impact of Training, 4832–4837.

56   Azman Ismail et al., "Supervisor's Role as an Antecedent of Training Transfer and Motivation to Learn in Training Programs," *Acta Universitatis Danubius: Oeconomica* 6, no. 2 (2010): 18–37, http://journals.univ-danubius.ro/index.php/oeconomica/article/view/614/565. Creative Commons License: https://creativecommons.org/licenses/by/4.0/.

57   Barbara Greenstein, May 26, 2017.

58   Azman Ismail et al., "Supervisor Communication in Training Program: an Empirical Study in Malaysia," *Management & Marketing* 7, no. 1 (2009): 59–68, http://www.mnmk.ro/documents/2009/5_Azman%20Malaezia_FFF.pdf. Creative Commons License: https://creativecommons.org/licenses/by/4.0/.

59   Office of Disability Employment Policy, U.S. Department of Labor, "Employee Assistance Programs for a New Generation of Employees: Defining the Next generation," https://www.dol.gov/odep/documents/employeeassistance.pdf.

60   Office of Disability Employment Policy, U.S. Department of Labor, "Employee Assistance Programs."

61   Scott H. Silverman, interview by Sylvia Melena, November 13, 2017. I interviewed Scott H. Silverman, CEO of Confidential Recovery, an outpatient program in San Diego, California, allowing clients to continue their careers or jobs and enjoy living at home while receiving long-term therapy. Scott is the recipient of numerous honors and awards, an acclaimed speaker, an expert in workforce development, and the author of *Tell Me No, I Dare You: A Guide for Living a Heroic Life*. For more information about Scott and Confidential Recovery, please visit https://www.confidentialrecovery.com/.

62   Scott H. Silverman, November 13, 2017.

63   Scott H. Silverman, November 13, 2017.

64   Scott H. Silverman, November 13, 2017.

65   Scott H. Silverman, November 13, 2017.

66   Scott H. Silverman, November 13, 2017.

67   U.S. Department of Labor. *FMLA (Family & Medical Leave)*. https://www.dol.gov/general/topic/benefits-leave/fmla.

68   U.S. Department of Labor. *FMLA (Family & Medical Leave)*.

69   Ann Clayton, *Workers' Compensation: a Background for Social Security Professionals, Social Security Bulletin* 65, no. 4. (2003-2004),

https://www.ssa.gov/policy/docs/ssb/v65n4/v65n4p7.html.

70   Ann Clayton, *Workers' Compensation.*

71   United States Department of Justice, Civil Right Division. *Information and technical assistance on the Americans with Disabilities Act.* https://www.ada.gov/ada_intro.htm.

Chapter 9 – The Power of Employee Recognition

72   Janine Victor and Crystal C. Hoole, "The Influence of Organisational Rewards on Workplace Trust and Work Engagement," *SA Journal of Human Resource Management* 1, no. 0, (2017): 1–14, https://sajhrm.co.za/index.php/sajhrm/article/view/853. Creative Commons License: https://creativecommons.org/licenses/by/4.0/.

73   Kartinah Ayupp and Then Hsiao Chung, "Empowerment: Hotel Employees' Perspective," *Journal of Industrial Engineering and Management* 3, no. 3 (2010): 561–575, http://www.jiem.org/index.php/jiem/article/view/166/81. Creative Commons License: https://creativecommons.org/licenses/by/3.0/.

74   Janine Krüger and Chantal Rootman, "How Do Small Business Managers Influence Employee Satisfaction and Commitment?," *Acta Commercii* 10, no. 1 (2010): 59–72, http://www.actacommercii.co.za/index.php/acta/article/viewFile/114/114. Creative Commons License: https://creativecommons.org/licenses/by/4.0/.

75   Janine Victor and Crystal C. Hoole, "The Influence of Organisational Rewards," 1–14.

76   Janine Krüger and Chantal Rootman, "How Do Small Business Managers," 59–72.

77   Jorunn Theresia Jessen, "Job Satisfaction and Social Rewards in the Social Services," *Journal of Comparative Social Work* 5, no. 1 (2010): 1–18, http://journal.uia.no/index.php/JCSW/article/view/215/150. Creative Commons License: https://creativecommons.org/licenses/by/4.0/.

78   Vida Škudienė, Karolina Šlepikaitė, and James Reardon, "Front-Line Employees' Recognition and Empowerment Effect on Retail Bank Customers' Perceived Value," *Journal of Service Science* 6, no. 1 (2013): 105–116, https://doi.org/10.19030/jss.v6i1.8241. Creative Commons License: https://creativecommons.org/licenses/by/3.0/.

79   Vida Škudienė, Karolina Šlepikaitė, and James Reardon, "Front-Line Employees' Recognition," 105–116.

80   Jerry P. Haenisch, "Factors Affecting the Productivity of Government Workers," *SAGE Open* 2, no. 1 (2012): 1–7, https://doi.org/10.1177/2158244012441603. Creative Commons License: https://creativecommons.org/licenses/by/3.0/.

81   W.P. Brick, personal communication, November 7, 2017. I interviewed Wendi Brick, President & CEO of Customer Service Advantage, Inc. and author of *The Science of Service: Six Essential Elements for Creating a Culture of Service in the Public Sector.* Wendi's life work is advancing world-class customer service in the public sector. For more information, please visit www.thecsaedge.com.

82   Wendi Brick, November 7, 2017.

Chapter 10 – The 4 P's of Accountability™

83   Schalk W. Grobler and Yvonne du Plessis, "Requisite Leader Behavioural Competencies for Sustainable Organisational Performance," *Acta Commercii* 16, no. 1 (2016): 1–8, http://dx.doi.org/10.4102/ac.v16i1.347. Creative Commons License: https://creativecommons.org/licenses/by/4.0/.

84   Rita Maria Silva, António Caetano, and Qin Zhou, "(In)justice Contexts and Work Satisfaction: The Mediating Role of Justice Perceptions," *International Journal of Business Science and Applied Management* 7, no. 1 (2012): 15–28, http://www.business-and-management.org/download.php?file=2012/7_1-15-28-Silva,Caetano,Zhou.pdf. Creative Commons License: https://creativecommons.org/licenses/by/3.0/.

85   Rita Maria Silva, António Caetano, and Qin Zhou, "(In)justice Contexts," 15–28.

86   Rita Maria Silva, António Caetano, and Qin Zhou, "(In)justice Contexts," 15–28.

87   Rita Maria Silva, António Caetano, and Qin Zhou, "(In)justice Contexts," 15–28.

88   Kaisa Perko et al., "Back to Basics: The Relative Importance of Transformational and Fair Leadership for Employee Work Engagement and Exhaustion," *Scandinavian Journal of Work and Organizational Psychology* 1, no. 1, 6 (2016): 1–13. http://doi.org/10.16993/sjwop.8. Creative Commons License: https://creativecommons.org/licenses/by/4.0/.

89   Kaisa Perko et al., "Back to Basics," 1–13.

90   Kaisa Perko et al., "Back to Basics," 1–13.

Chapter 11 – Boosting Performance through Progressive Discipline

No notes.

Chapter 12 – The Case for Documentation

No notes.

Chapter 13 – Final Wrap-up: Practical Application

No notes.

Bibliography

Ahmed, Ishfaq, Wan Khairuzzaman Wan Ismail, Salmiah Mohamad Amin, Muhammad Ramzan, and Talat Islam. "A Literary Look at Outcomes of Support at Work." *Research Journal of Applied Sciences, Engineering and Technology* 5, no. 12 (2013): 3444–3449. http://maxwellsci.com/print/rjaset/v5-3444-3449.pdf. Creative Commons License: https://creativecommons.org/licenses/by/3.0/.

Ayupp, Kartinah and Then Hsiao Chung. "Empowerment: Hotel Employees' Perspective."*Journal of Industrial Engineering and Management* 3, no. 3 (2010): 561–575. http://www.jiem.org/index.php/jiem/article/view/166/81. Creative Commons License: https://creativecommons.org/licenses/by/3.0/.

Blaga, Monica and Nico W. Van Yperen. "Easy and Difficult Performance-Approach Goals: Their Moderating Effect on the Link Between Task Interest and Performance Attainment." *Psychologica Belgica* 48, no. 2–3 (2008): 93–107. http://doi.org/10.5334/pb-48-2-3-93. Creative Commons License: https://creativecommons.org/licenses/by/4.0/.

Carter, J.D. Tony. "Managers Empowering Employees." *American Journal of Economics and Business Administration* 1, no. 2 (2009): 41-46. http://thescipub.com/PDF/ajebasp.2009.41.46.pdf. Creative Commons License: https://creativecommons.org/licenses/by/4.0/.

Chullen, Cody Logan. "How Does Supervisor Burnout Affect Leader-Member Exchange? A Dyadic Perspective." *International Business & Economics Research Journal* 13, no. 5 (2014): 1113–1126. https://doi.org/10.19030/iber.v13i5.8777. Creative Commons License: https://creativecommons.org/licenses/by/3.0/.

Clayton, Ann. "Workers' Compensation: a Background for Social Security Professionals." *Social Security Bulletin* 65, no. 4 (2003-2004). https://www.ssa.gov/policy/docs/ssb/v65n4/v65n4p7.html (accessed: September 22, 2017).

245

Grobler, Schalk W. and Yvonne du Plessis. "Requisite Leader Behavioural Competencies for Sustainable Organisational Performance." *Acta Commercii* 16, no. 1 (2016): 1–8. http://dx.doi.org/10.4102/ac.v16i1.347. Creative Commons License: https://creativecommons.org/licenses/by/4.0/.

Haenisch, Jerry P. "Factors Affecting the Productivity of Government Workers." *SAGE Open* 2, no. 1 (2012): 1–7. https://doi.org/10.1177/2158244012441603. Creative Commons License: https://creativecommons.org/licenses/by/3.0/.

Heiberger, Richard M. and Naomi B. Robbins. "Design of Diverging Stacked Bar Charts for Likert Scales and Other Applications." *Journal of Statistical Software* 57, no. 1 (2014): 1–32. https://www.jstatsoft.org/article/view/2132. Creative Commons License: https://creativecommons.org/licenses/by/3.0/.

Hussain, Tajammal and Sheikh Sana ur Rehman. "Do Human Resource Management Practices Inspire Employees' Retention?" *Research Journal of Applied Sciences, Engineering and Technology* 6, no. 19 (2013): 3625–3633. http://maxwellsci.com/print/rjaset/v6-3625-3633.pdf. Creative Commons License: https://creativecommons.org/licenses/by/3.0/.

Ismail, Azman, Sofiah Bongogoh, Sheela Chitra Chandra Segaran, Rodney Gavin, and Rabaah Tudin. "Supervisor Communication in Training Program: an Empirical Study in Malaysia." *Management & Marketing* 7, no. 1 (2009): 59–68. http://www.mnmk.ro/documents/2009/5_Azman%20Malaezia_FFF.pdf. Creative Commons License: https://creativecommons.org/licenses/by/4.0/.

Ismail, Azman, Hasan Al Banna Mohamed, Ahmad Zaidi Sulaiman, and Suriawati Sabhi. "Supervisor's Role as an Antecedent of Training Transfer and Motivation to Learn in Training Programs." *Acta Universitatis Danubius: Oeconomica* 6, no. 2 (2010): 18–37. http://journals.univ-danubius.ro/index.php/oeconomica/article/view/614/565. Creative Commons License: https://creativecommons.org/licenses/by/4.0/.

Jessen, Jorunn Theresia. "Job Satisfaction and Social Rewards in the Social Services." *Journal of Comparative Social Work* 5, no. 1 (2010): 1–18. http://journal.uia.no/index.php/JCSW/article/view/215/150. Creative Commons License: https://creativecommons.org/licenses/by/4.0/.

Krüger, Janine and Chantal Rootman. "How Do Small Business Managers Influence Employee Satisfaction and Commitment?" *Acta Commercii* 10, no. 1 (2010): 59–72. http://www.actacommercii.co.za/index.php/acta/article/viewFile/114/114. Creative Commons License: https://creativecommons.org/licenses/by/4.0/.

Lucian, Isac Florin, Rusu Sergiu, and Cureteanu Radu Silviu. "Problems in Measuring Customer Satisfaction." Analele Universității Constantin Brâncuși din Târgu Jiu: Seria Economie 2, no. 4 (2012): 23–25. http://www.utgjiu.ro/revista/ec/pdf/2012-04.II/3_Isac%20Florin,%20Rusu%20Segiu%20,Cureteanu%20Radu%201.pdf. Creative Commons License: https://creativecommons.org/licenses/by/4.0/.

Office of Disability Employment Policy, U.S. Department of Labor. "Employee Assistance Programs for a New Generation of Employees: Defining the Next Generation." https://www.dol.gov/odep/documents/employeeassistance.pdf.

Perello-Marin, M. Rosario and Gabriela Ribes-Giner. "Identifying a Guiding List of High Involvement Practices in Human Resource Management." *WPOM-Working Papers on Operations Management* 5, no. 1 (2014): 31–47. https://polipapers.upv.es/index.php/WPOM/article/view/1495. Creative Commons License: https://creativecommons.org/licenses/by/4.0/.

Perko, Kaisa, Ulla Kinnunen, Asko Tolvanen, and Taru Feldt. "Back to Basics: The relative importance of transformational and fair leadership for employee work engagement and exhaustion." *Scandinavian Journal of Work and Organizational Psychology* 1, no. 1 (2016): 1– 15. http://doi.org/10.16993/sjwop.8. Creative Commons License: https://creativecommons.org/licenses/by/4.0/.

Qian, Jing, Bin Wang, Zhuo Han, and Baihe Song. "Ethical Leadership, Leader-Member Exchange and Feedback Seeking: a Double-Moderated Mediation Model of Emotional Intelligence and Work-Unit Structure." *Frontiers in Psychology* 8, no. 1174 (2017): 1–11. https://doi.org/10.3389/fpsyg.2017.01174. Creative Commons License: https://creativecommons.org/licenses/by/4.0/.

Rus, Mihaela. "Transformational Leadership Type in Public and Private Organizations." *EIRP Proceedings* 7, no. 1 (2012): 588–594. http://www. proceedings.univ-danubius.ro/index.php/eirp/article/view/1246/1225. Creative Commons License: https://creativecommons.org/licenses/by/4.0/.

Silva, Rita Maria, António Caetano, and Qin Zhou. "(In)justice Contexts and Work Satisfaction: The Mediating Role of Justice Perceptions." *International Journal of Business Science and Applied Management* 7, no. 1 (2012): 15–28. http://www.business-and-management.org/download.php?file=2012/7_1–15-28-Silva,Caetano,Zhou.pdf. Creative Commons License: https://creativecommons.org/licenses/by/3.0/.

Škudienė, Vida, Karolina Šlepikaitė, and James Reardon. *"Front-Line Employees' Recognition and Empowerment Effect on Retail Bank Customers' Perceived Value."* *Journal of Service Science* 6, no. 1 (2013): 105 – 116. https://doi.org/10.19030/jss.v6i1.8241. Creative Commons License: https://creativecommons.org/licenses/by/3.0/.

Stinglhamber, Florence, Géraldine Marique, Gaëtane Caesens, Donatienne Desmette, Isabelle Hansez, Dorothée Hanin, and Françoise Bertrand. "Employees' Organizational Identification and Affective Organizational Commitment: An Integrative Approach." *PLoS ONE* 10, no. 4 (2015): 1–23. https://doi.org/10.1371/journal.pone.0123955. Creative Commons License: https://creativecommons.org/licenses/by/4.0/.

United States Department of Justice, Civil Right Division. "Information and technical assistance on the Americans with Disabilities Act." https://www. ada.gov/ada_intro.htm (accessed: September 22, 2017).

U.S. Department of Labor. "FMLA (Family & Medical Leave)." https://www. dol.gov/general/topic/benefits-leave/fmla (accessed: September 22, 2017).

Van Yperen, Nico W., Monica Blaga, and Tom Postmes. "A Meta-Analysis of Self-Reported Achievement Goals and Nonself-Report Performance across Three Achievement Domains (Work, Sports, and Education)." *PLoS ONE* 9, no. 4 (2014): 1–16. https://doi.org/10.1371/journal.pone.0093594. Creative Commons License: https://creativecommons.org/licenses/by/4.0/.

Victor, Janine and Crystal C. Hoole. "The Influence of Organisational Rewards on Workplace Trust and Work Engagement." *SA Journal of Human Resource Management* 1, no. 0, (2017): 1–14. https://sajhrm.co.za/index.php/sajhrm/article/view/853. Creative Commons License: https://creativecommons.org/licenses/by/4.0/.

Zia, Haleema, Hafiz Muhammad Ishaq, Salma Zahir, and Faiz Ahmed. "To Investigate the Impact of Training, Employee Empowerment and Organizational Climate on Job Performance." *Research Journal of Applied Sciences, Engineering and Technology* 7, no. 22 (2014): 4832–4837. http://www.maxwellsci.com/msproof.php?doi=rjaset.7.872. Creative Commons License: https://creativecommons.org/licenses/by/3.0/.

Made in the USA
Coppell, TX
09 March 2020